D0380330

The LEGAL SYSTEM

OPPOSING VIEWPOINTS®

Other Books of Related Interest

The LEGAL SYSTEM

OPPOSING VIEWPOINTS®

Laura K. Egendorf, *Book Editor*

Daniel Leone, *President*
Bonnie Szumski, *Publisher*
Scott Barbour, *Managing Editor*

OPPOSING
VIEWPOINTS®
SERIES

GREENHAVEN
PRESS ®

THOMSON
———— ✳ ————
GALE

San Diego • Detroit • New York • San Francisco • Cleveland
New Haven, Conn. • Waterville, Maine • London • Munich

THOMSON

————★————™

GALE

© 2003 by Greenhaven Press. Greenhaven Press is an imprint of The Gale Group, Inc., a division of Thomson Learning, Inc.

Greenhaven® and Thomson Learning™ are trademarks used herein under license.

For more information, contact
Greenhaven Press
27500 Drake Rd.
Farmington Hills, MI 48331-3535
Or you can visit our Internet site at http://www.gale.com

LIBRARY OF CONGRESS CATALOGING-IN-PUBLICATION DATA

Egendorf, Laura K., 1973–
    The legal system : opposing viewpoints / Laura K. Egendorf, book editor.
        p. cm.
    Includes bibliographical references and index.
    ISBN 0-7377-1231-7 (pbk. : alk. paper) —
    ISBN 0-7377-1232-5 (hardcover : alk. paper)
        1. Justice, Administration of—United States—Juvenile literature. I. Title.
    KF8700.Z9 E44 2003
    347.73—dc21   2001008679

Printed in the United States of America

"Congress shall make
no law...abridging the
freedom of speech, or of
the press."

First Amendment to the U.S. Constitution

The basic foundation of our democracy is the First
Amendment guarantee of freedom of expression.
The Opposing Viewpoints Series is dedicated to the
concept of this basic freedom and the idea that it is
more important to practice it than to enshrine it.

Contents

Why Consider
Opposing Viewpoints?

"The only way in which a human being can make some approach to knowing the whole of a subject is by hearing what can be said about it by persons of every variety of opinion and studying all modes in which it can be looked at by every character of mind. No wise man ever acquired his wisdom in any mode but this."

John Stuart Mill

In our media-intensive culture it is not difficult to find differing opinions. Thousands of newspapers and magazines and dozens of radio and television talk shows resound with differing points of view. The difficulty lies in deciding which opinion to agree with and which "experts" seem the most credible. The more inundated we become with differing opinions and claims, the more essential it is to hone critical reading and thinking skills to evaluate these ideas. Opposing Viewpoints books address this problem directly by presenting stimulating debates that can be used to enhance and teach these skills. The varied opinions contained in each book examine many different aspects of a single issue. While examining these conveniently edited opposing views, readers can develop critical thinking skills such as the ability to compare and contrast authors' credibility, facts, argumentation styles, use of persuasive techniques, and other stylistic tools. In short, the Opposing Viewpoints Series is an ideal way to attain the higher-level thinking and reading skills so essential in a culture of diverse and contradictory opinions.

In addition to providing a tool for critical thinking, Opposing Viewpoints books challenge readers to question their own strongly held opinions and assumptions. Most people form their opinions on the basis of upbringing, peer pressure, and personal, cultural, or professional bias. By reading carefully balanced opposing views, readers must directly confront new ideas as well as the opinions of those with whom they disagree. This is not to simplistically argue that everyone who reads opposing views will—or should—change his or her opinion. Instead, the series enhances readers' understanding of their own views by encouraging confrontation with opposing ideas. Careful examination of others' views can lead to the readers' understanding of the logical inconsistencies in their own opinions, perspective on why they hold an opinion, and the consideration of the possibility that their opinion requires further evaluation.

Evaluating Other Opinions

To ensure that this type of examination occurs, Opposing Viewpoints books present all types of opinions. Prominent spokespeople on different sides of each issue as well as well-known professionals from many disciplines challenge the reader. An additional goal of the series is to provide a forum for other, less known, or even unpopular viewpoints. The opinion of an ordinary person who has had to make the decision to cut off life support from a terminally ill relative, for example, may be just as valuable and provide just as much insight as a medical ethicist's professional opinion. The editors have two additional purposes in including these less known views. One, the editors encourage readers to respect others' opinions—even when not enhanced by professional credibility. It is only by reading or listening to and objectively evaluating others' ideas that one can determine whether they are worthy of consideration. Two, the inclusion of such viewpoints encourages the important critical thinking skill of objectively evaluating an author's credentials and bias. This evaluation will illuminate an author's reasons for taking a particular stance on an issue and will aid in readers' evaluation of the author's ideas.

It is our hope that these books will give readers a deeper understanding of the issues debated and an appreciation of the complexity of even seemingly simple issues when good and honest people disagree. This awareness is particularly important in a democratic society such as ours in which people enter into public debate to determine the common good. Those with whom one disagrees should not be regarded as enemies but rather as people whose views deserve careful examination and may shed light on one's own.

Thomas Jefferson once said that "difference of opinion leads to inquiry, and inquiry to truth." Jefferson, a broadly educated man, argued that "if a nation expects to be ignorant and free . . . it expects what never was and never will be." As individuals and as a nation, it is imperative that we consider the opinions of others and examine them with skill and discernment. The Opposing Viewpoints Series is intended to help readers achieve this goal.

David L. Bender and Bruno Leone,
Founders

Greenhaven Press anthologies primarily consist of previously published material taken from a variety of sources, including periodicals, books, scholarly journals, newspapers, government documents, and position papers from private and public organizations. These original sources are often edited for length and to ensure their accessibility for a young adult audience. The anthology editors also change the original titles of these works in order to clearly present the main thesis of each viewpoint and to explicitly indicate the opinion presented in the viewpoint. These alterations are made in consideration of both the reading and comprehension levels of a young adult audience. Every effort is made to ensure that Greenhaven Press accurately reflects the original intent of the authors included in this anthology.

Introduction

"Truth-seeking is an imperfect process. . . . If mistakes are to be made, they should be made in the direction of making sure that an innocent person is not convicted."

—*Jay M. Feinman*, Law 101: Everything You Need to Know About the American Legal System

One of the keystone responsibilities of the American legal system is to ensure that every defendant receives a fair trial. However, the perfection of DNA tests have recently proven that on numerous occasions people were arrested and convicted of crimes they did not commit. The results of these tests point out that the legal system is imperfect.

DNA, or deoxyribonucleic acid, is the genetic code that determines an individual's physical characteristics. It can be found in the nucleus of every cell. Because everyone has a unique DNA code (except identical multiple births), forensic testing on hair, semen, or blood left at a crime scene may determine whether a defendant committed the crimes for which he or she has been accused.

Law professor Barry Scheck has advocated using DNA in ambiguous cases in a nationwide effort he calls the Innocence Project, which provides free legal assistance for inmates who have proven that DNA testing may make a difference in the outcome of a retrial. The project has helped exonerate more than thirty-five prisoners. In an interview with the television program *Frontline*, Scheck stated, "This is total system failure. We're not talking about some procedural due process matter, some matter of unfairness in the way the trial was conducted. We're talking about people who are actually innocent. And that has to command our respect and attention and concern unlike any other kind of case."

DNA testing has, in effect, called into question more traditional evidence in determining guilt such as eyewitness testimony. Eyewitness testimony leads to an average of seventy-seven thousand arrests every year. Studies have found that faulty eyewitness testimony is a leading cause of false convictions. A 1997 report by the Constitutional Rights Foundation states, "Researchers at Ohio State University examined hundreds of wrongful convictions and determined that roughly 52 percent of the errors resulted from eyewitness mistakes." According to Boston defense attorney James Doyle, thirty-six of the first forty prisoners who were released after DNA testing had been convicted because of eyewitness testimony.

Several ways that eyewitnesses have been asked to identify suspects may compound the inaccuracy of their testimony. Criminal lineups, for example, seem to result in the witness selecting the person who most closely resembles the person he or she saw, regardless of whether the actual perpetrator is in the lineup. Other factors include the amount of time that passed between the crime and the identification, as well as police and prosecutors influencing the eyewitness. Race also affects an eyewitness's ability to successfully identify a suspect. Studies have found that people are 15 percent more likely to accurately identify suspects of their own race.

The behavior of police can also affect a person's ability to receive a fair trial. Despite the presence of Miranda laws—which have largely eliminated physical and psychological torture of suspects—many critics of the police contend that defendants are compelled into confessing to crimes they did not commit. For example, Earl Washington was convicted of murder in 1984 and sentenced to death; he was later exonerated by DNA testing. Washington's lawyers argued during his murder trial that his IQ of 69 had made it easier for police to lead him into a false confession. In an article for *American Prospect*, Alexander Nguyen writes, "[The] tactics police departments have developed are so effective that police have even been able to extract false confessions from innocent suspects—a baffling phenomenon, but evidence that interrogations have continued to be psychologically compelling." These tactics can include lying to a suspect about an accomplice's confession or the existence of witnesses and evidence.

The problem of wrongful convictions is one of the many issues facing the American legal system. In *The Legal System: Opposing Viewpoints*, the authors examine these issues in the following chapters: What Is the State of the American Civil Justice System? Does the Jury System Work? Is the Criminal Justice System Fair? What Should Be the Role of the Media in the Legal System? In those chapters, the authors consider how to achieve the idea: treating all citizens equally in the eyes of the law.

CHAPTER 1

What Is the State of the American Civil Justice System?

Chapter Preface

One criticism of the American civil justice system is that plaintiffs in civil suits sometimes receive unduly large settlements. Supporters of tort reform, which limits the types of disputes that can be taken to court and places caps on settlements, charge that these lawsuits damage the U.S. economy. However, other commentators maintain that these settlements are rare and involve circumstances that their critics ignore.

Lawsuits are much more common in the United States than in other industrialized nations. According to Californians Against Lawsuit Abuse (CALA), forty thousand product liability lawsuits are filed each year in America, compared to two hundred such suits in the United Kingdom. CALA also notes that the United States has thirty times as many lawsuits per person as Japan. In 1999, the median award for these lawsuits was $1.8 million. CALA charges that the costs of these suits are eventually passed on to the consumer "in terms of higher prices for products and services." Secretary of Energy Spencer Abraham, in his report "The Case for Legal Reform" (written when he was a U.S. senator from Michigan), writes: "Litigation adds 2.5 percent to the average cost of a new product in America." According to Abraham, the threat of liability lawsuits can also cause companies to shy away from developing new products.

However, not everyone agrees that these lawsuits are a significant problem. According to a study by the National Center for State Courts, of the nation's seventy-five largest counties, only 364 of 762,000 cases resulted in punitive damages. Additionally, the number of liability suits has decreased 9 percent since 1986. An editorial in the *Minneapolis Star Tribune* asserts that various studies prove "civil jurors are deliberative, responsible and anything but spendthrifts."

Opponents of tort reform often cite one of the most famous product liability suits—the woman who sued McDonald's when she spilled its coffee on her lap—as proof that the media and tort reform supporters misrepresent these cases. The coffee caused third-degree burns and required the eighty-one-year-old woman to undergo skin grafts. Although a jury initially awarded the woman $2.9 million, a judge reduced the amount to $600,000. In addition, she was not the only person to have been scalded by dangerously hot McDonald's coffee. More than seven hundred consumers were burned by the restaurant's coffee between 1982 and 1992, but those incidents were largely settled out of court.

In the following chapter, the authors consider the condition of the American civil justice system, including whether tort reform is necessary.

"In recent years, innumerable individuals have asserted all manner of rights that would have once been considered quixotic."

Frivolous Lawsuits Are a Problem in the Civil Justice System

Jodie Allen

In the following viewpoint, Jodie Allen asserts that the civil courts are filled with lawsuits filed by people who seek to establish absurd rights. According to Allen, these purported rights include the right to be protected from one's own mistakes and the right to be protected from various problems and irritations of life. She contends that although not all of these suits are successful, the proliferation of such frivolous cases have led to increased costs for consumers and benefit only the trial lawyers. Allen is a senior writer for *U.S. News & World Report*. Her articles have also appeared in *New Republic*.

As you read, consider the following questions:
1. Why does Allen jokingly blame Thomas Jefferson for the explosion of the tort industry?
2. What do legal positivists say gives worth to rights, as stated by the author?
3. According to Allen, what was the suggestion offered by the Committee for Economic Development to reform lawsuits against the insurance industry?

As we call the roll of debts owed the Founding Fathers on July 4, we might want to add one that is frequently overlooked: the birth of America's vibrant and fast-growing tort industry. As with so many of our cherished rights, much of the credit goes to Thomas Jefferson. When drafting the Declaration of Independence, Jefferson was under considerable time pressure. And, of course, he had to deal with that committee of fellow Founders. (What a bother that can be.) So, when it came to enumerating those "unalienable rights" with which we are all endowed, he took a shortcut—ticking off just a few illustrative examples and passing the burden of defining other rights on to future generations: "among these are Life, Liberty and the Pursuit of Happiness."

Asserting New Rights

Ever since, Americans have been struggling to complete that list. And in recent years the project has accelerated, thanks to the burgeoning ranks and growing ingenuity of the nation's trial lawyers, who stand ready to identify and extrapolate any unalienable prerogative as yet unrecognized. Granted, the assertion of individual rights has become an almost global phenomenon. But the tendency to define as a defensible right what other nationalities might view as a mere preference or desire is quintessentially American. Consider, for example, the title of a newsletter that has pursued me unbidden for several years: "The Right of Aesthetic Realism to Be Known." It's not "The Aesthetic Realism Report" or even "Some Things You Might Like to Know About Aesthetic Realism" but a legalistic demand that attention be paid.

Of course, as legal positivists like to point out, a right isn't worth much if no power enforces it. And it is hard to imagine that even an American judge would entertain a claim by the aesthetic realists against whatever force is denying them a hearing. Still, in recent years, innumerable individuals have asserted all manner of rights that would have once been considered quixotic. And some have even gotten them enforced. (You can monitor such cases at Overlawyered.com.)

Some recent assertions cluster under the rubric of the right to be protected from your own folly: an airline is blamed for the drunken rage of a passenger; a lawyer sues Ford after the child he left in a van on a hot day dies of hyperthermia; an Oakland, California, bank robber sues the city when a tear-gas device hidden in his loot goes off. Other claims don't have even this much philosophical consistency— people don't want to be protected only from themselves, they want to be protected from life itself. For instance, the right to non-sticky candy (a toffee maker is sued for dental irritation); the right to bladder-friendly brew (a man at a concert sues the beer concession for damages arising from his embarrassing need to repeatedly retreat to the men's room); the right to heist if you're homeless (or at least to swipe shopping carts in San Francisco); the right to be fooled (Disneyland is sued for emotional distress by visitors whose kids spot cartoon characters out of costume); and the right to be scared but not too scared (asserted against the operator of a theme park's "haunted house").

Eliminating Frivolous Claims

We should launch a serious effort to clear away frivolous lawsuits. I have long advocated a "fairness rule" that would give trial judges discretion in frivolous suits to order the loser to pay the winner's legal fees. Frivolous claims are the most basic abuse of the legal system. They are an affront to the cause of justice and an irresponsible use of public resources. People who file such claims must be held accountable for their actions.

So, too, must their attorneys. In the 2000 presidential campaign, George W. Bush wisely opposed amending the Federal Rules of Civil Procedure to require mandatory sanctions against attorneys who file frivolous claims. He also proposed a "three-strikes" rule, under which an attorney who files three egregiously frivolous suits would be barred from practicing in federal courts for three years. That's a harsh sanction, but only the most persistently reckless lawyers need fear it.

Dan Quayle, *American Legion Magazine*, March 2001.

To be sure, not all claimants ultimately collect on their alleged damages. Once in a while a court declines even to consider an assertion of recompensable idiocy. For example, a judge threw out the damage claim of a man who, while drunk, climbed a high-voltage railroad tower. When a man went for a dip with a five-ton killer whale and didn't live to tell about it, his family sued SeaWorld—then thought better of it and withdrew the claim. (Perhaps they figured the whale would take the Fifth.) Still, you don't have some rights you probably thought you had. For example, the right to stomp in a mud puddle on purpose (in December 1999, a Florida youth was jailed for this offense). Or the right not to host rattlesnakes (a New York court made a realty company tear down a snakeproof fence in October 1999). On the other hand, the right to dunk parrots has now been firmly established, thanks to the acquittal of a Florida man charged with repeatedly dipping the head of his friend's bird in a tequila-laced drink. Sports is another area in which the march of new rights has stalled: in 1988, a retrograde federal judge told a tearful Virginia schoolgirl that "there is no constitutional right to play ball." A dozen years later, an Ohio magistrate declined legal protection for the right to win, dismissing a parent's suit against the coach of a boys' baseball team after a disastrous season.

The Costs of New Rights

But the trend is clearly in the other direction, given the emergence of, for instance, the right to be stopped before you kill again. Among the cases establishing that right: A California school administrator got a jury to award him $255,000 when a school district, relying on his job application, hired him despite his failure to disclose a prior sex-felony conviction. Similarly, in Ontario (the rights revolution has also taken hold north of the border—witness the recent right to strip suit filed by the 52-year-old "Toronto Torch"), a woman is suing two psychiatrists and her family doctor for failing to keep her from smothering her nine-year-old daughter. (The doctors reply that she was a recalcitrant patient who lied about her problems and refused medication.)

Naturally, rights proliferation doesn't come cheap—something old Tom and his fellow Founding Fathers may not have thought about when they left that vague "among these" statement in the Declaration. Today, the tort system's overhead costs (read: the fees that go to lawyers who try the cases) nearly equal the total compensation victims receive. That's why the Committee for Economic Development, a nonprofit business and civic group, recently proposed an intriguing reform scheme. The committee proposes to let consumers choose: they can buy low-cost insurance and guaranteed compensation for economic losses or medical costs alone, or they can keep their current insurance plans, along with the right to the uncertain pursuit of claims for pain, suffering, and other intangible damages.

You needn't worry that ideas like this will soon diminish your right to assert new and creative rights. The costs of the current system are diffuse—higher prices for insurance and almost everything we buy—while the benefits are concentrated in the pockets of trial lawyers, a politically powerful lobby that has provided generous support to President Clinton and other Democrats.

So if you're at the beach this Independence Day and some bully kicks sand in your face, don't head to the gym in search of biceps. Head to the courts in search of justice. True, the bully may counter that kicking sand is intrinsic to his pursuit of happiness. But, with a smart lawyer arguing your right to liberty from ophthalmic irritation, you should carry the day. And, when you do, you'll have Thomas Jefferson to thank.

*"Tort 'reform'. . . would skew the legal
system in favor of the powerful."*

Tort Reform Would Damage
the Civil Justice System

Robert S. Peck

In the following viewpoint, Robert S. Peck criticizes the efforts of corporate America and some state legislatures to limit Americans' ability to sue for injury. He argues that these attempts at tort reform would mar the justice system by skewing it in favor of powerful corporations at the expense of the plaintiffs. Peck also maintains that tort reform is a threat to constitutional government because it ignores the separation of powers that provides balance between the legislative and judicial branches. Peck is the Association of Trial Lawyers of America's senior director for Legal Affairs and Policy Research.

As you read, consider the following questions:
1. In Peck's view, what do "reform" advocates seek to accomplish?
2. What do tort-restriction laws limit, according to the author?
3. What does Peck believe will happen if concessions are made to tort restrictionists?

Excerpted from "Defending the American System of Justice," by Robert S. Peck, *Trial*, April 2001. Copyright © 2001 by Trial Magazine. Reprinted with permission.

As the battle over tort "reform" continues to ratchet up, the scholarship mustered in support of [Association of Trial Lawyers of America's] constitutional litigation program has proved a vital weapon. In all its challenges to state tort "reform" laws, the association has argued that they violate myriad constitutional guarantees, including the right to trial by jury, the right to a remedy, the bar on special legislation, the guarantees of equal protection and due process, and the single-subject rule. The scholarship that supported these arguments has helped achieve positive results.

In addition, ATLA lawyers have asserted that tort "reform" constitutes a threat to the fundamental principles of the separation of powers doctrine, an idea that was accepted by both the Illinois and Ohio Supreme Courts.

To understand why separation of powers can be a powerful argument against tort "reform," it is necessary to examine what upsets the business community about the existing, and frankly remarkable, legal system we enjoy in the United States and what it is that corporate America seeks to accomplish by "reforming" it.

Civil Justice Protects Individuals

Our civil justice system stands as a beacon of fairness in a world where clout and influence often predominate. Individuals who are neither wealthy nor well connected can bring huge multinational conglomerates into court to account for wrongful and injurious actions. Only in the courtroom, as opposed to legislative chambers or executive offices, can an individual seek full redress. There, injured people stand on an equal basis with powerful adversaries whose money, power, influential allies, campaign contributions, and lobbyists give them an undeniable advantage in the political system.

The advantages that unfairly tilt the political playing field in favor of powerful economic interests dissolve in a courtroom. There, the art of horse trading, the lure of lucre, and the ability to travel in influential circles count for nothing. Instead, decisions are made according to the facts and the rule of law.

Manufacturers often make purely economic decisions

about what constitutes an acceptable level of injury risk in their products. Our fundamental guarantee of access to justice ensures that a person harmed as a result of this crass calculation can seek compensation for that injury in a court of law, despite the considerable resources that can be mustered by the manufacturer and its insurance company against the lawsuit.

Little wonder, then, that corporate America rails against the civil justice system. Unscrupulous business barons mislead the press and the public by disseminating twisted anecdotes about "runaway" verdicts that paint an inaccurate picture of how juries render justice. These business leaders, who also deny responsibility for injuries their companies' products inflict on consumers, have put tort "reform" high on their public policy agenda.

The tort "reform"—or, more accurately and descriptively, tort restrictionism—they support, using the business community's outsized political clout, would skew the legal system in favor of the powerful. The advantages that business obtains in the political system are enlisted to create similar advantages in the legal system.

The Goals of Restrictionists

Rather than seek any proper reform of the system, tort restrictionism creates roadblocks to holding wrongdoers accountable. "Reform" advocates seek to impose caps on damage awards, create new costs and obstacles to the commencement of meritorious lawsuits, set higher burdens of proof for plaintiffs, fashion enhanced affirmative defenses for defendants and limitations on liability for joint tortfeasors, and abrogate venerable legal doctrines.

At its most basic and essential level, the tort-restrictionist agenda represents dissatisfaction with the legal system, especially judges and juries, on the part of those who are frequent defendants in personal injury cases. While dressed up in the rhetoric of nonexistent litigation explosions, insurance crises, horrifying economic consequences, unconscionable jury awards, and frivolous lawsuits, tort-restriction laws constitute little more than relief to the habitually negligent and the intentionally reckless.

Writing in 1992, in an exhaustive and detailed law review article, University of Iowa law professor Michael Saks concluded that the tort restrictionists' account of juries and the civil justice system is "built of little more than imagination." The fact that tort-restriction laws continued to be enacted in a time of unrivaled economic prosperity puts the lie to the various claims of need that have been asserted.

Oliver. © 1997 by Big Bend Sentinel. Reprinted by permission of Gary Oliver.

Tort restrictionists seek to slay dragons that do not exist. Their agenda attempts to hijack the civil justice system, turning it away from the objective of redressing grievances and making it suit their need to minimize liability for wrongdoing.

An Improper Role for Legislatures

Typically, when a legislature is amenable to entreaties from tort restrictionists, access to the legal system is transformed into a fire sale. Lobbyists for every industry realize their jobs depend on securing a niche for their clients' favorite legal protection.

When the legislature grants such largesse, it improperly takes on the role of superjudiciary, acting as an overseer for the courts. Fortunately, as ATLA's litigators have demonstrated in litigation challenging these laws, the very state constitutions that create the state legislatures stand as a bulwark against such an arrogation of power.

Tort-restriction laws do not regulate the substance of causes of action. Instead, these statutes limit the authority, responsibilities, and prerogatives of the judiciary—as well as its partner in the exercise of judicial power, the jury—while also substantially interfering with the rights of injured people to seek redress from the courts.

In Ohio, for example, the legislature explicitly asserted a new power of cancellation over recent constitutional decisions of that state's supreme court. The tort-restriction law also attempted to change rules of procedure and evidence, despite the Ohio constitution's exclusive grant of authority over these rules to the state supreme court. Similar issues about court rules were raised in the successful challenges to the Illinois and Florida tort "reform" laws. . . .

Not a Public Policy Choice

In defense of tort-restriction laws, we often hear the refrain that the courts owe great deference to the public policy choices of the legislature, as though the restriction of constitutional rights, the obliteration of the jury system, the destruction of fairness in the civil justice system, and the illicit arrogation of judicial power by the legislature are mere public policy choices that the legislature somehow has the right to make.

In so arguing, tort restrictionists have attempted to turn the separation of powers doctrine on its head by asserting that the courts owe an unexamined and one-way deference to any and all legislative actions, and they have labeled this attitude "cooperation." This argument for blanket deference makes no sense when the legislature has intruded into a constitutional realm reserved for the judiciary and has embarked on an uneducated journey to control the conduct of the state's judicial proceedings.

Past instances of judicial deference or adoption of legislatively initiated changes of the kind that tort-restriction laws attempt to effect do not change constitutions or their application. Deference does not transfer authority from one branch to another. While it is often in the public interest for the branches to cooperate, voluntary cooperation should not be taken as a surrender or diminution of the judiciary's exclusive authority.

What tort restrictionists want is nothing less than the elevation of the designs of today's transient legislature over the words and intent of those who framed each state's organic law. Concession would result in a creeping aggrandizement of legislative power, an annulment of the express words of the constitutions, and a transformation of the judiciary into a mere cipher, rather than a coequal branch.

Florida Chief Justice Edwin Randall, writing about Florida's 1868 constitution, trenchantly declared:

> If [the legislature could appropriate judicial authority to itself], the modern theories of government and the forms of civil governments framed in the later periods are but solemn complicated frauds, machines for the amusement and the impoverishment of the people. If all political and judicial supervisory power is lodged in one body of men, notwithstanding the establishments which all peoples have so reverently organized under written constitutions, which in terms divide the powers of government into several departments of magistracy, supposed to be created to perform the offices of adjustments and balances, then are such several departments mere cheats and shams, baubles and playthings invented to delude and ensnare.

Remembering Constitutional Law

In ruling tort-restriction laws unconstitutional, modern courts are reviving these once-forgotten lessons of constitutional law, history, and experience with the assistance of briefs that develop these themes. In Illinois, the supreme court struck down that state's omnibus tort-restriction law, declaring that "[i]n furtherance of the authority of the judiciary to carry out its constitutional obligations, the legislature is prohibited from enacting laws that unduly infringe upon the inherent powers of judges."

Earlier, the Washington Supreme Court had similarly held that "[a]ny legislative attempt to mandate legal conclusions would violate the separation of powers." And in Ohio, a sweeping tort-restriction law was found to be an "open challenge [to that state's supreme] court's authority to prescribe rules governing the courts of Ohio and to render definitive interpretations of the Ohio constitution binding upon the other branches."

These conclusions are nothing new. In his influential and authoritative treatise on constitutional law, written in 1868, Michigan Supreme Court Justice Thomas Cooley said:

> If the legislature cannot thus indirectly control the action of the courts, by requiring of them a construction of the law according to its own views, it is very plain it cannot do so directly, by setting aside their judgments, compelling them to grant new trials, ordering the discharge of offenders, or directing what particular steps shall be taken in the progress of a judicial inquiry.

The type of legislative interference with judicial (and jural) authority that tort-restriction laws represent cannot pass constitutional muster in a system of separated powers. Our constitutions are clear: The doors of our courts must be open to those seeking meaningful remedy for injury to person, property, or reputation. Tort-restriction laws slam those doors closed. ATLA's constitutional litigation program works to ensure that the courts appropriately kick them back open.

"My experience . . . has made me a believer in the importance of class actions."

Class Action Suits Benefit the Average Citizen

John H. Church Jr.

John H. Church Jr. details his successful experience with a class action suit in the following viewpoint. Church describes how he was fired after the company where he was employed was acquired by another firm. He sued on charges of age discrimination. He concludes that class action lawsuits help people who would lack the resources to take on large corporations by themselves. Church is a former employee of Emery Air Freight Corporation. This viewpoint was taken from testimony he gave before the House Judiciary Committee.

As you read, consider the following questions:
1. According to Church, how many days after the acquisition of Emery Air Freight Corporation was he fired?
2. What were some of the steps taken by the class action attorneys, as described by Church?
3. For how much money was the lawsuit settled, as stated by the author?

Excerpted from John H. Church Jr.'s testimony before the House Judiciary Committee, October 30, 1997.

My name is John H. Church, Jr. I live in Greer, South Carolina. I have been married for 30 years and have four children.

A Demoralizing Firing

In February, 1989, I was employed by Emery Air Freight Corporation as a Regional General Manager. I had been an employee of Emery for twenty-one and one-half years, and had worked my way up through the ranks. I was making $77,000 per year. I was 54 years old.

On February 17, 1989, Consolidated Freightways announced that it wanted to buy my Company, Emery Air Freight. For the acquisition to go forward, we employees had to vote in favor of the purchase because we owned all of Emery's preferred stock through our employee stock option plan. To persuade us to go along with the acquisition, Consolidated Freightways told us in writing that: "The Company . . . will continue to employ all employees employed by the Company under terms and conditions of employment substantially comparable to, and in any event no less favorable than, those existing immediately prior to the Effective Time."

Because of my seniority with the Company, I had the right to be fired only for good cause after a hearing with the Vice President for Human Resources. I also had the right to two weeks of severance for each year of employment, up to a maximum of 26 weeks.

I believed Consolidated Freightways' promises. As a result, I and other Emery employees agreed to tender our shares. The acquisition was completed on April 3, 1989.

Eight days later, on April 11, 1989, I was constructively discharged. I was given no hearing, and there was no cause. I was given no severance. I was replaced by a man in his thirties, with less experience and fewer qualifications.

My firing was demoralizing. I had given my heart and soul to the Company for decades, and done everything the Company had asked of me. I was consistently evaluated as one of Emery's best managers. They didn't fire me because I was a bad employee. . . . They fired me because of my age.

I was angry. I drove 90 miles to Charlotte, North Carolina, to the offices of the Equal Employment Opportunity

Commission (EEOC). I told them that I wanted to file a charge of age discrimination. The EEOC attorney told me that I would never win and that this type of thing happens all the time.

A More Efficient and Balanced System

By allowing plaintiffs to bring class actions, courts attempt to balance the conflicting goals of civil procedure. The ultimate goal, of course, is to carry out the policies and values of the substantive rules of law. When many individual plaintiffs each have relatively small claims, this can be done only through a class action. An airline passenger may pay a few dollars more for a plane ticket because the airlines illegally inflated the price of tickets, or a credit card holder may pay a few cents more when a bank miscalculates the interest rate. Because of the small size of the claims and the expense of litigation, it isn't worthwhile for any one of these consumers to sue the airlines or the bank. The collective loss of all passengers or all credit card users, though, is very large. By bringing one suit for all of the consumers, a class action makes sure that the laws against price-fixing or misrepresenting interest rates are carried out and the people who are injured by the wrongful conduct are compensated.

Aggregating small claims in a class action also serves the value of operating the litigation system efficiently. A class action always involves at least one issue of law or fact that is common to many claims, such as whether a gas tank was defective or the airlines were price-fixing. Examining and deciding that issue once is more efficient than doing it again and again in different cases.

Jay M. Feinman, *Law 101*, 2000.

Soon thereafter, I got a call from a former Emery colleague from Richmond, Virginia, who told me that he too had been fired and replaced by a younger person. He told me that Consolidated Freightways had done that to hundreds of Emery managers across the country. He told me that he had contacted a lawyer in Richmond, and asked me if I wanted to talk to the attorney and join the suit. I told him that I would be interested in speaking with the attorney, but that I could not afford to pay attorneys' fees or case costs.

The attorneys agreed to take the case on a contingency basis, only being paid if we prevailed. They also agreed to advance all costs of the suit. I told them to name me as a plaintiff. Five others from Kentucky, Georgia, Missouri, Illinois, and Connecticut soon also joined in.

The Richmond lawyer called a California law firm that was familiar with class actions and they filed a class action lawsuit on behalf of the hundreds of Emery managers to whom this had happened. We sued in Federal Court in San Francisco, California, near where Consolidated Freightways is based.

The lawsuit was filed in 1990 and went on for four years. I was deposed for three days. The questioning was difficult. Consolidated Freightways hired some of the best lawyers in the country.

I produced documents, and I answered written questions. I also worked closely with my attorneys, who deposed the officers of Consolidated Freightways and discovered that prior to the purchase offer being announced, Consolidated Freightways had already made its plan to slash severance, fire the older Emery managers, and replace them with younger people at lower salaries.

A Successful Experience

Our attorneys worked hard. They hired a professor of statistics from Duke and a business consultant from Philadelphia with expertise in the transportation industry to analyze our claims. In late 1992, a court-approved mediator held a several day mini-trial, where testimony was presented on videotape, documents were put forth, and extensive arguments made about all issues. Without good lawyers, we would have been crushed.

In early 1993, the case settled for $13.5 million. I received approximately $120,000.00. I was happy to get it. It covered my family's expenses during the years that it took me to get another job comparable to the one I had at Emery.

From the Settlement Fund, the attorneys were repaid the approximately $500,000 that they had paid out of their own pockets on our behalf. For their time and hard work, the attorneys were paid approximately $4 million in attorneys' fees, or approximately 30 percent of the recovery. The Class received $9 million.

After the case settled and the money was paid out to the class, members of the Class called me to thank me. One woman told me that the payment from the case changed her life.

My experience with this case has made me a believer in the importance of class actions. I did not have the resources to fight Consolidated Freightways on my own. The costs of the suit, including the costs of expensive expert statisticians, were just too high. By banding together, we were able to achieve justice. Without the class action, we would not have been as successful. I have spoken to at least one person who tried to sue on his own, but did not fare nearly as well.

For people like me of average means to have a chance against a big company when we have been wronged, we need the help of class actions.

Thank you for listening to me.

"Private attorneys general may be too willing to bring nonmeritorious suits if these suits produce generous financial rewards for them."

Class Action Suits Benefit Attorneys

Deborah R. Hensler et al.

In the following viewpoint, Deborah R. Hensler and the other authors assert that the only people who benefit from class action suits are the attorneys, not the consumers seeking redress for damages. They contend that because private attorneys often receive enormous fees when a suit is successful, they are too willing to bring suits without merit into the justice system. In addition, the authors argue that these attorneys encourage quick settlements at the expense of trials that adequately examine the facts and law, thereby providing little help to the plaintiffs and other affected consumers. Hensler is the Judge John W. Ford Professor of Dispute Resolution at Stanford University Law School, director of the Stanford Center on Conflict and Negotiation, and a senior fellow at the Rand Institute for Civil Justice.

As you read, consider the following questions:

1. According to supporters of class action lawsuits, as cited by the authors, how do those lawsuits serve an important public purpose?
2. According to Hensler and the other authors, why do few consumer class members actively monitor the behavior of their attorney?
3. What responsibilities have judges been given in class action suits, as stated by the authors?

Private class actions for money damages, particularly those lawsuits in which each class member claims a small loss but aggregate claimed losses are huge, pose multiple dilemmas for public policy. Many believe that these lawsuits serve important public purposes by supplementing the work of government regulators whose budgets are usually quite limited and who are subject to political constraints. Hence, these are sometimes called "private attorneys general" lawsuits. Consumer advocates argue that without the threat of such lawsuits, businesses would be free to engage in illegal practices that significantly increase their profits as long as no one individual suffered a substantial loss. This notion of the purpose of damage class actions is sharply contested. In our view, the evidence regarding the historical intent of damage class actions is ambiguous. But whatever the rulemakers may have intended, the corporate representatives whom we interviewed said that the burst of new damage class action lawsuits has played a regulatory role by causing them to review their financial and employment practices. Likewise, some manufacturer representatives noted that heightened concerns about potential class action suits have had a positive influence on product design decisions.

Benefiting Lawyers, Not Consumers

Relying on private attorneys to bring litigation for regulatory enforcement has important consequences. When class action lawsuits are successful, they may yield enormous fees for attorneys because fees are usually calculated as a percentage of the total dollars paid by defendants. So, attorneys have substantial incentives to seek out opportunities for litigation, rather than waiting for clients to come to them. Over the years, class action specialists have developed extensive monitoring strategies to improve their ability to detect situations that seem to offer attractive grounds for litigation. To spread the costs of monitoring, they look for opportunities to litigate multiple class action lawsuits alleging the same type of harm by different defendants or in different jurisdictions. Success in previous suits provides the wherewithal for investigating the potential for more and different types of suits—suits that test the boundaries of existing law. Thus, the financial incentives that damage class actions provide to private attorneys tend to drive the frequency and variety of class action litigation upwards. In our interviews, attorneys talked candidly about how these incentives operated in their practices and the practices of those who litigated against them. The key public policy question is whether the entrepreneurial behavior of private attorneys produces litigation that is, on balance, socially beneficial. Whereas public attorneys general may be reluctant to bring meritorious suits because of financial or political constraints, private attorneys general may be too willing to bring nonmeritorious suits if these suits produce generous financial rewards for them.

Lawyers' Fees Versus Cash Payments

	Class Counsel Award for Fees & Expenses ($M)	Total Cash Payment to Class Members ($M)
Consumer Class Actions		
Roberts v. Bausch & Lomb	$8.5000	$9.175[b]
Pinney v. Great Western Bank	$5.223	$11.232
Graham v. Security Pacific Housing Services, Inc.	$1.920	$7.583
Selnick v. Sacramento Cable	$0.511	$0.271
Inman v. Heilig-Meyers	$0.580	$0.272[c]
Martinez v. Allstate/Sendejo v. Farmers	$11.288	$8.914
Mass Tort Class Actions		
In re Factor VIII or IX Blood Products	$36.500[a]	$620.000[a]
Atkins v. Harcros	$24.900	$25.175
In re Louisiana-Pacific Siding Litigation	$25.200	$470.054[a]
Cox et al. v. Shell et al.	$75.000	$838.000[a]

[a]Projected.
[b]Estimated from financial reports and other public documents.
[c]Information not from public records.

Deborah R. Hensler et al., *Class Action Dilemmas: Pursuing Public Goals for Private Gain*, 1999.

Most consumer class members have only a small financial stake in the litigation. And, because of the way the class action rules are commonly applied, the class members may not even learn of the litigation until it is almost over. Even representative plaintiffs (i.e., those in whose name the suit is filed) may play little role in the litigation. As a result, there are few if any consumer class members who actively monitor the class action attorney's behavior. Such "clientless" litigation holds within itself the seeds for questionable practices. The powerful financial incentives that drive plaintiff attorneys to assume the risk of litigation intersect with powerful interests on the defense side in settling litigation as early and as cheaply as possible, with the least publicity. These incentives can produce settlements that are arrived at without adequate investigation of facts and law and that create little value for class members or society. For class counsel, the rewards are fees disproportionate to the effort they actually invested in the case. For defendants, the rewards are a less-expensive settlement than they may have anticipated, given the merits of the case, and the ability to get back to business rather than engage in continued litigation. For society, however, there are substantial costs: lost opportunities for deterrence (if class counsel settled too quickly and too cheaply), wasted resources (if defendants settled simply to get rid of the lawsuit at an attractive price, rather than because the case was meritorious), and—over the long run—increasing amounts of frivolous litigation as the attraction of such lawsuits becomes apparent to an ever-increasing number of plaintiff lawyers.

The Drawbacks of Increased Responsibility

Recognizing the potential for conflicts of interest in representative litigation, legal rulemakers have assigned judges special oversight responsibilities for class action litigation, including deciding class counsel's fees, and have devised other procedural safeguards as well. But procedural rules, such as the requirements for notice, judicial approval of settlements, and opportunities for class members and others to object to settlements, provide only a weak bulwark against self-dealing. Notices may obscure more than they reveal to class members. Fees may be set formulaically without regard to the value actually produced by the litigation. Whether class settlements are actually collected by class members or returned to defendants, whether the awards are in the form of cash or coupons, may receive little judicial attention. Those who might object to the settlement may not be granted sufficient time or information to make an effective case. Individuals who do step forward to challenge a less-than-optimal resolution or a larger-than-appropriate fee award may have a price at which they will agree to go away or join forces with the settling attorneys. Judges whose resources are limited, who are constantly urged to clear their dockets, and who increasingly believe that the justice system is better served by settlement than adjudication may find it difficult to switch gears and turn a cold eye toward deals that—from a public policy perspective—may be better left undone.

Our data do not provide a basis for estimating the proportion of litigation in which questionable practices obtain. But because both plaintiff class counsel and defense and corporate counsel related experiences to us pertaining to such practices, often in vivid terms, and because there is documentary evidence of such practices in some cases, we believe that they occur frequently enough to deserve policymakers' attention.

"Judges, and especially the justices of the high court, feel free to ignore the laws passed by others."

Activist Judges Undermine Democracy

Max Boot

Judges who make the law instead of interpreting it are harmful to democracy, Max Boot claims in the following viewpoint. According to Boot, these judges ignore the right of states to determine the best laws for their community in order to impose their own preferred viewpoints and policies. He also contends that federal judges display another type of activism by not overruling laws that give too much power to Congress and the president. Boot is the editorial features editor of the *Wall Street Journal* and the author of *Out of Order: Arrogance, Corruption, and Incompetence on the Bench*, the book from which the following viewpoint was excerpted.

As you read, consider the following questions:
1. What is a "juristocracy," as defined by Boot?
2. Why does the author believe that states' rights are central to the American system of government?
3. According to Boot, what fear animates the Supreme Court?

A merica used to be a democracy, a government of, by, and for the people. Now it has all the earmarks of a *juristocracy*, a government of, by, and for people who have attended law school. Judges have assumed unprecedented authority over our lives, usurping the powers once delegated to elected lawmakers, based on no solid grounding in the text of either a statute or the Constitution itself.

Three Myths About Judicial Activism

Because plaints about activism from the bench have been heard so often in recent decades, it's important to be specific about what we're objecting to—to wit, judges who rule based on their own preferences, not on the law. We should avoid becoming beguiled by three myths that are common in conservative circles:

First, it is not the case that judicial legislation began with the Warren Court. Even *Marbury v. Madison*—the 1803 ruling in which the Supreme Court for the first time declared an act of Congress unconstitutional and thus established the right of judicial review of legislation—has no real foundation in the text of the Constitution itself. Judges, no matter what their personal views, have always been tempted to make law, not interpret it, and not always with negative consequences.

Second, judicial activism is not strictly a liberal phenomenon. In the early years of this century, the Supreme Court was dominated by laissez-faire activists, and there are still a few conservative activist judges around.

Witness U.S. district judge Michael Hogan's decision blocking the implementation of a 1994 Oregon initiative legalizing physician-assisted suicide on the grounds that it was unconstitutional; this is as wrong-headed as Judge Henderson's actions in California. [Henderson blocked the implementation of Proposition 209.] Or there's U.S. district judge John E. Sprizzo's 1997 acquittal of two "pro-life" protesters on charges of blocking access to a Dobbs Ferry, New York, abortion clinic; the judge ruled that the men hadn't violated the law because they had acted out of religious, not criminal, motives. Good thing Judge Sprizzo didn't handle the trial of the World Trade Center bombers. Presumably, he would have let them go, too, because their terrorism had religious roots—in their case, radical Islamic views.

The third myth of the right is that judicial legislation is always wrong. Actually, in one area at least, legislating has always been the function of the judge, and so it should remain. This is the area of common law, the (state) law that today by and large governs contracts, torts, property, trusts, and estates. It would be extremely difficult, if not impossible, for a legislature to codify all the law in these areas; no legislature could anticipate every possible contingency in every case that may be filed. So judges, acting ostensibly on the basis of precedent but really on their own intuition, have to decide for themselves the rules in these areas on a case-by-case basis.

The classical commentators of the law, the Blackstones and Cokes, denied that judges legislated even in these areas. Their theory was that "a preexisting rule was there, imbedded, if concealed, in the body of the customary law. All that the judges did was to throw off the wrappings and expose the statue to our view." Since the advent of "legal realism" in the early twentieth century, hardly anybody hews to this view anymore. But legal realism—the realization that judges make up the law—is not an invitation to an open-ended legislative role. The judge, [Benjamin] Cardozo argues, "legislates only between the gaps. He fills the open spaces in the law." Cardozo goes on to note: "In countless litigation, the law is so clear that judges have no discretion. They have the right to legislate within gaps, but often there are no gaps."

This distinction, as crisp as a freshly printed magazine in Cardozo's mind, has gotten as blurred as a crumpled-up old newspaper with the passage of time. Justice Antonin Scalia argues that many of his brethren on the bench apply common-law techniques when they should instead be guided by the text of a statute or the Constitution itself.

Every student's first year in law school, notes Scalia, is spent playing common-law judge, "devising out of the brilliance of one's own mind, those laws that ought to govern mankind." Indeed, all American law students are taught based on the "case method": In a course on constitutional law, the students study *only* judges' rulings interpreting the Constitution; incredible as this may sound to a nonlawyer, our budding Blackstones *never* study the text of the Constitution itself. And many of these students don't lose the habit of common-law judging even when they join the Supreme Court, where their job is to interpret the law devised by legislators or the Founding Fathers, not to create their own.

"The [Supreme] Court," Scalia argues, "will distinguish its precedents, or narrow them, or if all else fails overrule them, in order that the Constitution might mean what it *ought* to mean." The rule, he suggests, is that "[i]f it is good, it must be so," which effectively reduces the Constitution to the level of common law. In short, judges, and especially the justices of the high court, feel free to ignore the laws passed by others and instead impose their own policy preferences in their decisions.

The Importance of States' Rights

While the expansion of judicial power has infringed upon democracy at all levels, the intrusion has been especially great at the state level. "States' rights" have largely been replaced with more nebulous, judicially created and judicially protected individual "rights." Today, alas, "states' rights" is a battle cry associated in many minds with the South's defense of slavery and segregation. It's high time to rescue this concept from the opprobrium into which it has sunk; states' rights lie at the very heart of the American system of governance. State governments, after all, are closer to the people than are the federal authorities in Washington. They can create laws better suited to local conditions, and by a political version of natural selection, the best solutions will wind up being replicated elsewhere. "It is one of the happy incidents of the federal system," Justice [Louis] Brandeis famously noted, "that a single courageous State may, if its citizens choose, serve as a laboratory; and try novel social and economic experiments without risk to the rest of the country." To give only one example of many: Wisconsin pioneered welfare reform measures that, in 1996, were implemented nationwide by Congress.

Another fortunate feature of federalism is that it contains a natural check on any state's going too far and enacting policies that are either counterproductive or downright tyrannical: Unhappy residents can always vote with their feet. If you don't like the high taxes and large government of New York, you can move to Utah, and if you don't like Utah's lack of amenities and regulations, you can move to New York. It's more difficult, however, for you to leave the country to protest the intrusiveness of the national government.

How Congress Can Prevent Judicial Activism

• Congress should exercise its power to limit the jurisdiction of the courts. The Constitution provides that Congress is authorized to establish those federal courts subordinate to the Supreme Court and set forth their jurisdiction. Congress also has the power to limit the jurisdiction of the Supreme Court and regulate its activities. Accordingly, Congress should exercise this authority to restrain an activist judiciary.

• Congress should stop the federalization of crime and the expansion of litigation in federal courts. Too often it is Congress that enlarges the power and authority of the federal courts and provides more opportunities for judicial activism by enacting new federal criminal statutes or creating new federal causes of action. By restraining its own law-making powers, Congress can also help to rein in the federal courts.

Edwin L. Meese III, *Hoover Digest*, no. 4, 1997.

Federalism not only offers an excellent approach to safeguarding liberty and good government but also holds the key to social peace. In all multiethnic, multicultural nations there is great danger of minorities feeling oppressed by the majority, whether it's the Quebeçois in Canada or the Bosnian Muslims in the old Yugoslavia. Under the federalist system, minority groups—the Mormons, say—can enjoy a high level of self-determination at the state level, thus dissipating separatist pressures. The success of the federalist model can be measured by the more than 130 years of internal peace we've enjoyed since the Civil War. No wonder federalism is being widely adopted around the globe, from the European Union to Russia.

Yet at the same time, federalism is under siege in America. Under our federalist blueprint, the Constitution spells out certain "limited and enumerated powers" for the federal government and reserves all the rest to the states via the Tenth Amendment: "The powers not delegated to the

United States by the Constitution, nor prohibited by it to the States, are reserved to the States respectively, or to the people." If the juristocracy respected the Founders' intentions, it would rule along the lines suggested by one scholar: "Any truly new thing done by the federal government is unauthorized and therefore void," while "[a]ny truly new thing done by a state must be outside of those prohibitions, and must, therefore, be constitutional." Instead, the courts' tendency is nearly the opposite: to clamp the states in judicial irons, while giving Uncle Sam freedom to do anything he likes.

Efforts to Limit Authority

When it comes to federal legislation, the juristocracy's activism —if it can be labeled as such—takes the form of *not* acting. Federal judges have always been more loath to override Congress—which, after all, pays their salaries and staffs— than the state legislatures. Indeed, after *Marbury v. Madison* in 1803, the Supreme Court apparently didn't overrule another act of Congress for fifty-four years (in the infamous *Dred Scott* case); but many more state statutes fell by the wayside.

This tendency to give great leeway to Washington, but not to Albany or Austin, grew more pronounced after 1937. President Franklin Roosevelt threatened to add new justices to the Supreme Court in order to stop the conservative court from overturning New Deal legislation, as it had done in the past. Although the court-packing scheme was defeated, the justices suddenly saw the light, and in the famous "switch in time that saved nine," began rubber-stamping all future New Deal legislation. In the blink of an eye, the justices had gone from overturning too many federal laws to approving too many—a trend that only now, six decades later, is starting to abate.

The Court effectively refused to enforce any constitutional limits on the central government's authority by shoehorning every possible expansion of federal fiat under the Commerce Clause ("The Congress shall have Power . . . To regulate Commerce with foreign nations, and among the several states, and with the Indian Tribes") or the Necessary and Proper Cause ("The Congress shall have Power . . . To make all Laws which should be necessary and proper for carrying into Execution the foregoing Powers, and all other Powers vested by this Constitution in the Government of the United States, or in any Department or Officer thereof").

It was only in 1995 that the Court finally suggested, however gingerly, that the federal government had exceeded its enumerated authority. That realization was confirmed in 1997, when the justices overturned the Brady Act and the Religious Freedom Restoration Act on the grounds that Congress didn't have the power to run roughshod over the states in those areas. (It is also only in the last few years that the high court has rediscovered traditional property rights— as opposed to newfangled rights such as a "right" to welfare benefits or public housing—which had generally been written out of the Constitution since the 1930s.)

Ironically, these modest attempts to impose some limits on Congress' authority have led some critics to label *this* Supreme Court as "activist." But this is pure sophistry, coming, as this criticism usually does, from the biggest fans of liberal judicial activism. Is it really activism for the Rehnquist Court to respect the status quo ante, namely, to show more respect for states' rights than some of its recent predecessors have done? Is it really activism for the Court to strike down *any* statute at all, no matter how clearly unconstitutional? I think not.

When the Court has struck down acts of Congress in recent years, the justices have usually been on solid ground. In 1976, for instance, the Supreme Court struck down most of a draconian campaign finance law on the grounds that capping political spending would be akin to capping political speech, which clearly isn't permissible under the First Amendment. More recently in 1997, the Court overturned, also on First Amendment grounds, the Communications Decency Act, which would have regulated all Internet content in a futile attempt to keep "indecent" material from kids.

With both the campaign finance and Internet cases, it took a flagrant violation of the Constitution for the Supreme Court to overturn an act of Congress—and in both instances, the justices displayed a high degree of unanimity in their findings. These were not instances of the justices substituting their own policy preferences for those of the Founders. Indeed, the more conservative members of the Court who voted to strike down the Communications Decency Act in all likelihood would have voted to approve it had they sat in Congress. They must have overturned the law with reluctance, and only because it so clearly conflicted with the Constitution. Had the justices *not* overturned those statutes, they would have been guilty of activism—ruling based on politics, not the law. . . .

Outlawing State Puritanism

The courts have been especially eager to strike down state laws on social and cultural issues—issues where there is a great chasm between the opinions of the chattering classes (the so-called opinion leaders who spout off in leading newspapers and on Sunday television talk shows) and the Bible Belt traditionalists. Guess whose side judges take in this culture war?

H.L. Mencken defined "Puritanism" as "the haunting fear that someone, somewhere might be happy." The Supreme Court seems to be animated at times by the haunting fear that someone, somewhere might be puritanical. Hence its diktats that nowhere, nohow, under no circumstances must any state restrict the availability of contraceptives or abortion before the point of "viability." So, too, the high court's prohibition of the time-honored practice of prayer in public schools, or even the invocation of God at public school graduations. (It's a sign of how the courts defer to the federal government that the justices allow official prayers every day on the floor of Congress.) And then, of course, there are the Court's pornography cases, which allow communities to ban only material deemed "obscene," not stuff that excites "normal, healthy sexual desires."

Virtually the only bow the Court has made in recent years to benighted notions of morality was upholding a Georgia antisodomy law, but in light of the justices' 1996 decision overturning a Colorado anti–gay rights initiative, even antisodomy laws may soon be relegated to the courts' trash bin.

We have a federalist Constitution precisely in order to allow conservative states to enact puritanical ordinances, whereas liberal states may take a more libertine path. This allows Americans of differing viewpoints—some traditional, others cosmopolitan—to live in whatever area makes them most comfortable. By striking down so many state laws, the courts are upsetting this delicate balance and undermining the foundations of American democracy.

"We must try to keep the judiciary as free as possible from the partisanship to which it has been subjected."

Congress Is a Threat to Judicial Independence

Herman Schwartz

In the following viewpoint, Herman Schwartz argues that Republican legislators during the Clinton presidency posed a danger to judicial independence. He maintains that these senators and representatives prevented judicial candidates whom they considered to be too activist from being named to fill vacancies on the bench. According to Schwartz, these conservative politicians focus wholly on the political views of liberal candidates while ignoring the many instances in which a conservative justice ignored or effectively rewrote the Constitution. He concludes that while activism can occasionally go too far, it is important to maintain judicial independence. Schwartz is a professor of law at American University in Washington, D.C., and the author of *Packing the Courts: The Conservative Campaign to Rewrite the Constitution.*

As you read, consider the following questions:

1. In 1996, as stated by Schwartz, how many trial judges made it through the Senate?
2. According to the author, how did the conservative majority on the Supreme Court rewrite the 11th Amendment?
3. What are examples cited by Schwartz of how activism has occasionally gone too far?

From "One Man's Activist . . . ," by Herman Schwartz, *The Washington Monthly*, November 1997. Copyright © 1997 by The Washington Monthly Company. Reprinted with permission.

Judges, watch your backs: The congressional Republicans have officially declared war on "judicial activists," judges who go beyond interpreting the law into the realm of what GOP lawmakers consider "making" the law. Rep. Bob Barr of Georgia is but one of several Republicans to denounce the current crop of jurists for "assuming for themselves the powers and responsibilities of legislators or executives"—an offense those on the right say must not be treated lightly. They have been particularly incensed over a few decisions setting aside death sentences, excluding evidence in a drug case, and blocking the implementation of the California referendum ending affirmative action programs. [In May 1997,] Barr joined Majority Whip Tom DeLay of Texas in calling for the impeachment of judges as a "proper tool" for "political offenses," with an impeachable offense defined by DeLay as "whatever a majority of the House of Representatives considers it to be at a given moment in history." Their stated goal, according to DeLay: "The judges need to be intimidated."

Judicial Appointments Have Been Hijacked

With an eye toward weeding out future judicial activists, GOP senators have virtually hijacked the appointment process. Judiciary Committee Chairman Orrin Hatch has declared he will not "stand by to see judicial activists named to the federal bench." To this end, Hatch and his fellow Republicans have instituted a massive slowdown on judicial appointments. According to political scientist Sheldon Goldman of the University of Massachusetts, who has been studying the nomination process for 40 years, the Republicans are engaged in an effort "unprecedented in its scope . . . to deny the Clinton administration as many nominations as possible."

Among their favorite tactics is the imposition of increasingly intrusive requests for the nominee's opinions. For example, [in 1996] Margaret Morrow, the first woman to serve as president of the California Bar Association, was unanimously approved by the Senate Judiciary Committee. Because of Republican footdragging, however, Morrow's nomination didn't come up for a floor vote during the 1996 session. Moreover, when the Senate reconvened [in 1997,]

Republican Charles Grassley of Iowa demanded Morrow's position on every one of 160 California initiatives in the last 10 years. (Grassley eventually scaled back his demands—after all, how much intimidation is necessary?)

Other GOP legislators have pushed for even more direct action to keep "activists" off the bench. Sen. Slade Gorton of Washington tried unsuccessfully to have Congress cut into the president's nominating power by requiring the president to get advance approval for a judicial candidate's ideology from the senators representing the circuit to which the candidate would be nominated. For his part, Sen. Phil Gramm of Texas pledged to block a Clinton nominee on the basis that the person had been "politically active."

Such delaying tactics have already borne fruit. In all of 1996, the Senate let through only 17 trial judges and no appellate judges, an unprecedentedly small number. [1997's] Congress seems to be following the same route: As of September 30, the Senate had confirmed just 18 judges, leaving 96 vacancies on the federal bench—including around 30 that the Administrative Office of the United States Courts calls "judicial emergencies," judgeships unfilled for more than 18 months. Some slots have been vacant since 1994. For a while, President Clinton provided the Republicans with a convenient excuse for the outrageous number of vacancies by sending up very few nominations. However, this cover is no longer available, as the president has now nominated some 70 judges, many originally sent up during the last Congress.

The conservative crusade against activist judges has been even more effective on the state level, where elective judges who voted in ways displeasing to Republicans have been denied re-election by organized electoral campaigns. In Tennessee, for example, Judge Penny J. White heard only one death penalty case in her 19 months on the state Supreme Court. In that case, she voted with her colleagues to order a new death-sentence hearing for a convicted murderer. Less than two months later, she was denied reappointment in a routine retention election, the victim of a Tennessee Republican Party campaign against her. Likewise, Nebraska Supreme Court Justice David Lanphier was ousted [in

November 1998] for having voted against a term-limits law and in favor of a retrial for some defendants convicted of second-degree murder.

The result of the conservative campaign is a massive pile-up in the federal courts. On the West Coast, oral arguments in some 600 cases were canceled last year, and the Second Circuit in New York has had to cancel sittings as well. One trial judge in Illinois put all of his civil cases on hold and went an entire year hearing only criminal cases, while a San Diego district court holds only about 10 civil trials a year.

The Republicans justify themselves by arguing that the damage they're inflicting is all in the name of defending the constitutional separation of powers against judicial activism. But oddly enough, Republican crusaders seem to have over-looked an important point: Some of the worst "activist" of-fenders on the bench today are the conservative members of the Supreme Court.

Throwing Out the Constitution

Despite DeLay and company's condemnation of judges who they say "have thrown out the Constitution" in favor of their own wisdom, over the years, it is the Supreme Court's con-servatives who have frequently done just that.

For example, in the 1976 case *Nat'l League of Cities v. Usery*, Chief Justice William Rehnquist (then an associate justice) succeeded in coalescing a majority to overturn federal legislation requiring state and local governments to meet the minimum-wage and maximum-hours provisions of the Fair Labor Standards Act. Unable to rely on any constitutional text, Rehnquist invoked vague notions of "state sovereignty."

More recently, [in June 1997] the five conservative jus-tices on the court overturned the Brady Gun Control bill be-cause it required local sheriffs to do a background check on a prospective gun purchaser. As in the *Nat'l League of Cities* case, the conservative justices conceded that they could not actually derive any limitations on federal power from the text of the 10th Amendment, which simply "reserves" to the states the "powers not delegated to the United States." As Justice [Sandra Day] O'Connor admitted, this is "essentially a tautology," because the amendment says nothing about what powers are in fact reserved. Instead, the justices relied solely on their own conception of what "state sovereignty" and "the federal structure" entail.

The Foundations of Judicial Independence

There are two constitutional foundations for judicial independence, and either might be violated by a legislative action.

First, separation of powers protects judicial independence. At the federal level and in every state, the judiciary is a co-equal branch of government. Justice Lewis Powell explained that the doctrine of separation of powers can be violated in two ways: "One branch may interfere impermissibly with the other's performance of its constitutionally assigned function. Alternatively, the doctrine may be violated when one branch assumes a function that more properly is entrusted to another."

Second, due process of law—both procedural and substantive—provides a basis for constitutional protection of judicial independence. Legislative actions that deny a meaningful hearing before a neutral decision maker violate procedural due process. The Supreme Court has long declared that the very essence of due process of law is a fair hearing before an impartial decision maker.

Erwin Chemerinsky, *Trial*, November 1998.

In some cases, the conservative majority has gone so far as to openly rewrite constitutional text. The 11th Amendment to the Constitution explicitly excludes from the federal judicial power only suits "against one of the United States by citizens of another State." Nevertheless, [in 1995] the court's conservatives rewrote the amendment to also exclude suits against a state by its own citizens—in the process overruling a recent precedent, and overturning a federal statute. And [in 1997,] the court overturned the Religious Freedom Restoration Act, a law passed unanimously in the House and by a 97-3 vote in the Senate, which sought to expand protection for religious freedom, particularly for minority sects.

An Indifference to States' Rights

Of course, in the current antigovernment climate, the argument that the justices are simply curtailing federal power in order to honor states' rights is a popular one. It is also flawed. Take the issue of affirmative action: Since 1978, when the Bakke case involving the University of California's decision to set aside 16 out of 100 places for minorities at the Davis School of Medicine was decided, conservatives have voted to strike down virtually every affirmative action plan to come before the court, regardless of whether the plan was adopted by state or federal legislators or officials. Until 1989, they failed except with respect to employee layoffs. With the arrival of Justice Kennedy in 1988, however, the balance shifted, and with its ruling on the 1989 Richmond, Va., case, the Supreme Court struck down some 236 state and local affirmative action plans.

Another example of this indifference to states' rights is the area of criminal justice. Since the Nixon appointees took over in 1972, the conservative majority has steadily cut into the Warren Court decisions establishing rights for the accused. Disregarding its long-standing policy not to hear state cases involving federal constitutional questions if those cases could be decided under state law, the court has reached out to overturn decisions of more liberal state courts.

What becomes increasingly clear from the court's record is that conservative justices are not so much concerned with strict adherence to the Constitution as with promoting conservative values. In none of the aforementioned cases, or numerous others like them, has the conservatives' purported zeal for judicial restraint or states' rights prevented them from riding roughshod over state and local legislation or court rulings that they disagreed with. And although the court's liberals have joined conservatives in some of their most controversial rulings, like overturning the Religious Freedom Restoration Act, even Clint Bolick's Institute for Justice has admitted that the court's conservatives are more inclined to strike down both federal and state laws than Clinton's two appointees, Ruth Bader Ginsburg and Stephen Breyer.

A Changing Debate

So why aren't Messrs. Hatch, DeLay, Barr, and their friends threatening to impeach the high court's most active "activists"? Simple: Like their conservative counterparts on the courts, congressional Republicans don't object to "judicial activism" per se. They simply oppose "liberal judicial activism." As one federal judge put it, "The Republicans define 'activist' according to their political agenda. It's OK to be an activist if you're striking down affirmative action and gun-free school laws." Or, as American Bar Association President and staunch conservative N. Lee Cooper puts it: "Activism [is] a phrase that, like beauty, seems to be in the eye of the beholder. It is fair to say that for the most vocal critics in today's debate, judicial activism is conveniently tossed around as a means of condemning any position that doesn't fit the critic's ideological mold."

In fact, the political debate over "judicial activism" has undergone a 180-degree turn in the last 70 years. During Franklin Roosevelt's administration, when the largely conservative Supreme Court was striking down New Deal legislation, liberals were up in arms about jurists' overstepping their constitutional bounds. And upon being named to the court, FDR appointee Justice Felix Frankfurter adhered to a strict policy of judicial restraint, reflecting his belief that the court should, whenever possible, defer to the will of the people as expressed through the legislature.

Today, of course, it's the conservatives who are up in arms. Their current campaign against "liberal judicial activists" is part of an ideological struggle that began in earnest as a reaction to the transformation of American life that started in the 1950s: the increased openness and freedom; the refusal of those outside the favored circle of power and privilege—women, blacks, homosexuals—to stay in their place; the ever-more powerful role of government in social and economic matters, and concomitant with that, the implicit devaluation of the rugged, Darwinian individualist. The federal courts were crucial to these changes, making them a natural target for the backlash. The "Impeach Earl Warren" signs that went up all over the South in the wake of the Brown school desegregation decision were among the first expressions of that reaction.

The Federal Bench in the Reagan-Bush Years

With the Reagan Revolution of 1981, the anti-court forces went into high gear. After numerous legislative failures, Edwin Meese and other die-hard conservatives decided that the only way to radically change American law was by tilting the federal bench sharply to the right. They went at it systematically, focusing on the Supreme Court and intermediate appellate levels where federal law is made. Men (and an occasional woman) from the far right of the judicial spectrum were appointed en masse. Such well-known and not-so-well-known conservatives as Sandra Day O'Connor, Anthony Kennedy, Antonin Scalia, Clarence Thomas, Robert Bork, Richard Posner, and Kenneth Starr were appointed—without objection, in all but a few cases. (Two notable exceptions are Bork's and Thomas' appointments to the Supreme Court—though not their appointments to the circuit court.) Potential nominees were asked their views on abortion, school prayer, unions, and other controversial matters. Moderates like Republican Judith Whittaker, who made the mistake of supporting the Equal Rights Amendment; and Philip Lacovara, one of Washington's most distinguished attorneys who, though a Goldwater supporter, joined a lawyers' civil rights group, were vetoed. Independents like Deputy Solicitor General Andrew Frey, who had given $25 to a gun-control group, were also rejected.

The result was a transformation of the federal judiciary as 12 years of Reagan-Bush appointees put solid conservative majorities on almost all the federal courts. The only court that remained relatively free of conservative domination for much of this period was the Supreme Court, because Justice Lewis Powell—most of the time a conservative vote—not infrequently swung over to the liberal side on key issues like affirmative action. That came to an end with the arrival of Anthony Kennedy who, with a few notable exceptions, has consistently voted with the Rehnquist-Scalia-Thomas-O'Connor bloc.

Bill Clinton's victory in 1992 and a Democratic Senate gave liberal Democrats a chance to restore some balance to the federal courts. The Republicans, though in the minority in 1993–94, threatened to challenge nominees they considered too liberal. Clinton's response was to avoid nominating judges who could be labeled as clearly liberal. As a result, a recent study by three political scientists found that the Clinton judges are less liberal than President Jimmy Carter's and quite similar to those of President George Bush, except that there are more minorities and women among the Clinton group.

Then came the Republican takeover of the Senate in 1994. Now, Clinton's judicial nominees and appointees alike find themselves under attack for their "liberal activism"—despite the fact that conservative activists like Clint Bolick have conceded that Clinton's nominees have been "moderate."

Good and Bad Activism

Truth be told, all judges are "activist." They have to be, particularly in constitutional cases. To last more than a few years, a constitution must be written in what Chief Justice John Marshall called "great outlines" that specify only "its important objects," outlines that must be filled in by judges. This is particularly true of our Constitution, written over 200 years ago by people whose vision was shaped by an America very different from the one in which we live today. After all, *Brown v. Board of Education* was one of the most "activist" decisions in our history. Would we have wanted it to come out differently?

Moreover, all constitutions and most statutes are the product of compromises, many of which are deliberately ambiguous in order to paper over differences that cannot be bridged, only bypassed. When these deliberately ambiguous texts come to the courts, the latter have no choice but to "make" the law.

Activism can, of course, go too far—though what is "too far" is often disputable and usually depends on who wins or loses. It is generally agreed that the pre–New Deal conservative judges were too aggressive, and these days a vociferous minority of our population believes that the *Roe v. Wade* court was as well. By and large, however, the system has managed to keep this activism within accepted limits. Many of the liberal activist "horrors" cited by DeLay et al., for example, were reversed by higher courts, rightly or wrongly. And if the mainstream of the nation believes the courts have gone too far, history shows that sooner or later the offending rulings will be modified or overruled.

Independence Must Be Preserved

The important thing is to maintain judicial independence. For that, we must try to keep the judiciary as free as possible from the partisanship to which it has been subjected. The House Judiciary Committee, for instance, has held hearings on a proposed constitutional amendment to eliminate the life tenure for federal judges that is the precondition for their independence. And Judge Robert Bork shocked even his allies with a proposal to allow a majority of either house of Congress to overrule federal or state court decisions.

Of course, some partisanship is inevitable, especially at the Supreme Court level. A conservative president can naturally be expected to nominate somewhat conservative judges, and vice-versa. What has kept the system running smoothly in the past has been the understanding that it is the president's prerogative to nominate any jurist he feels has the intellectual mettle to do the job well. And by and large, Democrats went along with the Reagan-Bush appointments. (In fact, during Bush's final year in the White House, the Democrat-controlled Senate approved 66 judicial appointments.) In order for an ideological balance to be maintained in the courts, the Congress must respect the will of the people—as expressed through their elected president—where judicial appointments are concerned. That's the way the system is supposed to work. By trying to win the whole game, the Republicans are gumming up the works. It is they, in fact, and not the judges they are attacking, who are betraying our constitutional heritage "in order to advance their own political views."

Periodical Bibliography

The following articles have been selected to supplement the diverse views presented in this chapter.

Max Boot	"Lies in Our Courtrooms," *American Enterprise*, May/June 1999.
Cathleen Burnett	"'Frivolous' Claims by the Attorney General," *Social Justice*, Summer 1998.
Erwin Chemerinsky	"When Do Lawmakers Threaten Judicial Independence?" *Trial*, November 1998.
Robert P. George and Ramesh Ponnuru	"Courting Trouble," *National Review*, August 17, 1998.
Issues and Controversies on File	"Judicial Activism," September 12, 1997.
Kenneth Jost	"The Federal Judiciary," *CQ Researcher*, March 13, 1998.
Jay Lefkowitz	"A Modest Tort Proposal," *Weekly Standard*, August 16, 1999.
Eric Longley	"Judicial Nullification," *Liberty*, August 1999.
Edwin L. Meese III	"How Congress Can Rein in the Courts," *Hoover Digest*, no. 4, 1997.
Robert M. O'Neil	"Assaults on the Judiciary," *Trial*, September 1998.
Dan Quayle	"The Trouble with Tort," *American Legion*, March 2001.
Lawrence W. Reed	"Taxation by Litigation Threatens Every American Business," *Freeman: Ideas on Liberty*, September 1999.
Lawrence W. Schonbrun	"The Class Action Con Game," *Regulation*, Fall 1997.

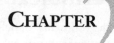

CHAPTER 2

Does the Jury System Work?

Chapter Preface

When the American colonies revolted against England, they did not reject every element of English life. One example of the continuing British influence is the role of the jury in the U.S. legal system.

The right to a trial by jury was established in 1215 in the *Magna Carta*, a document that developed out of a conflict between King John and rebellious nobles. In the thirty-ninth clause of that document, the king promised: "No free man shall be taken or imprisoned . . . or outlawed or exiled or in any way destroyed, nor will we go or send against him, except by the lawful judgment of his peers or by the law of the land." Although early jurors also served as witnesses, by the fifteenth century the sole purpose of jurors was to judge the facts of a case based on the evidence presented before them.

The jury system was brought over to the American colonies. One case that shows the importance of juries in the colonies was the trial of printer John Peter Zenger in 1735 on charges of libel against the British government. Despite the instructions of the judge, the jury acquitted Zenger, helping to establish freedom of the press in America. Less than six decades later, the Bill of Rights codified the importance of trial by jury. The Sixth Amendment requires that a defendant in a criminal case have his or her case heard by an impartial jury, while the Seventh Amendment ensures that parties in a civil case whose monetary value is over twenty dollars will also be permitted a trial by jury.

The American jury system has changed over the years. In 1875, racial discrimination in the jury selection process became a criminal offense, although that did not prevent Southern states from finding ways to exclude African Americans, such as requiring that only registered voters—a group that excluded African Americans—could serve as jurors. Discrimination against female jurors continued into the twentieth century; the Supreme Court ruled in 1941 that women could be excluded from federal jury lists. While overt discrimination no longer exists in the jury system, debate persists on whether peremptory challenges enable lawyers to select jurors based on race and gender. Other reforms have included the introduction of nonunanimous verdicts and allowing jurors to question witnesses.

Although it has been in place for hundreds of years, whether the American jury system is in need of reform remains in contention.

"Many of the problems in our criminal justice system, . . . are tied to the use of juries."

The Jury System Should Be Reformed

William T. Pizzi

The jury system is in need of reform, William T. Pizzi contends in the following viewpoint. According to Pizzi, the current jury system has caused many of the problems in the criminal justice system. He argues that several changes should be made, including eliminating peremptory challenges, allowing for greater user of nonunanimous verdicts, and replacing all-citizen juries with a mix of citizens and judges. Pizzi is a professor at the University of Colorado Law School in Boulder and the author of *Trials Without Truth*, from which the following viewpoint has been excerpted.

As you read, consider the following questions:
1. Why does Pizzi believe American trials lack focus?
2. What does the author think would be the benefits of replacing juries with mixed panels of citizens and judges?
3. According to the author, how do juries complicate appellate reviews?

For the last decade the American public has been told over and over by bar leaders that our trial system is basically sound and that whatever problems have emerged in recent trials they are isolated occurrences that can be attributed largely to human error. . . . The problems in the system are structural. They are not going to go away and, indeed, they are likely to get worse over time as citizens become more cynical about the system. In this [viewpoint,] I want to review some of the structural problems in the system and discuss the issues that must be faced if we are to reform it.

Truth Is Not a Priority

A strong trial system has to place a high priority on truth and work hard to achieve that goal. Our trial system does not do this and, as a result, our trials lack focus. Without a clear goal to work toward, trial judges cling tightly to procedure almost as an end in itself because they have nothing else to guide them and are unsure in what direction the trial should go. In this situation a lawyer who sees adversarial advantage in a confusing, prolonged, and bitterly contentious trial finds it easy to create such a trial.

A trial, be it more or less adversarial, is simply a way of testing the evidence that has been gathered during the investigation in order to determine whether or not the defendant is guilty of the crime. Trial systems can vary considerably in the way they carry out this task. But the goal of the system has to be the same: an accurate and reliable evaluation of the evidence in order to determine the defendant's guilt. . . .

A Complicated System

The [jury] system is extremely complicated and intimidating for citizens. Nevertheless we want our fact finders to be citizens who come in off the street with no prior experience in the courtroom and almost no preparation for the task, which they are expected to carry out perfectly. A prospective juror who has had prior experience on a jury is often disqualified for service by one of the lawyers. Second, it is extremely difficult for citizens with other obligations and responsibilities to serve on a jury in the United States because it is hard to estimate how long the trial may take, particularly if the case is an important one. Because the judge has imperfect knowledge of the evidence in the case he cannot easily predict its length. Also, hearings within the trial can arise unpredictably, often causing jurors to spend hours midtrial in the jury room wondering what is going on in the courtroom. Third, while preferring fact finders who have never done any fact-finding, misplaced American populism results in a trial system that gives the jurors much less advice and help from the judge than they get in other trial systems.

Jurors Have Difficulty Judging Expert Witnesses

Jurors can be bowled over by, or wrongly put off by, experts who claim that they know things beyond the jury's ken. Ordinary witnesses are found to be honest or dishonest, confident or heedless, dispassionate or reckless by the jurors' commonsense standards. Such witnesses are evaluated much as a person would evaluate a casual acquaintance. But expert witnesses are—well, experts. Some may be discounted, but it is not easily done. Jurors know little about science, and especially about the important scientific principle that a scholar never overstate or exaggerate a finding. When an expert witness speaks confidently of what "science" knows and admits of few, if any, exceptions to this "knowledge," the juror, as Kent Scheidegger has put it, is "at sea without a sextant." They are often at a loss to know how or whether to discount these claims, a fact clearly revealed in the first Menendez trial. Expert witnesses may be accepted by juries for the same reasons—manner, personality, appearance—that juries accept lay witnesses. But the best scientists may have a gruff manner, an unappealing personality, and an unattractive appearance; in science, personal attributes count for nothing in justifying a scientific claim. Jurors will not know that lay and expert witnesses must be judged by different standards.

James Q. Wilson, *Moral Judgment*, 1997.

Our jury system needs to be reformed. An immediate reform should be to cut down or even eliminate peremptory challenges, protecting against "the unreachable juror" by permitting jury verdicts that are not unanimous. Oregon and Louisiana have permitted nonunanimous verdicts for some time and there is plenty of support for nonunanimous verdicts in other countries. I have also argued that American judges should be required to give juries much more help than they do at present by reviewing and summarizing the evidence for the jury at the end of the trial. Admittedly, this is controversial as the judge may be able to influence the jury in its decision to some extent. But this is an issue that needs to be confronted. If almost all continental countries use mixed panels of professional and lay judges to decide a defendant's fate and if most common law countries at least permit the trial judge to review the evidence for the jury, do we really have that much to fear in allowing a judge to discuss the evidence with the jury? When we have got to the point where even judges talk about jury trials as "rolling the dice," isn't it time to rethink the relationship of the judge and jury in the United States?

I would prefer to move away from juries composed solely of citizens in favor of mixed panels of judges and citizens. Perhaps skeptics will be reassured if we make sure that there are a sufficient number of citizens to outvote the professional judges. What is important is not the voting ratio but getting someone on the jury with knowledge of the law, experience in the system, and experience in fact-finding. I recognize that this proposal is controversial and runs up against American populism. But for all our rhetoric about juries, the present system shows in many, many ways that it doesn't really trust them.

Changes Are Overdue

Many of the problems in our criminal justice system, such as the extremes of advocacy and our incredibly complicated evidence rules, are tied to the use of juries. Juries also complicate appellate review of the decision at trial, be it an acquittal or a conviction, because there is no formal way of knowing the reasoning that went into the verdict. For all these reasons, some changes are overdue in the way citizens participate as fact finders at trial, or, at least, in the relationship between judges and juries.

> *"The broad attacks on the civil jury are premised on the most corrosive lie that can be told to a democratic society."*

The Jury System Is Under Attack

Jeffrey Robert White

In the following viewpoint, Jeffrey Robert White contends that the American judicial and legislative branches have tried to marginalize the civil jury system. According to White, the Supreme Court has given judges the power to reduce jury awards and prevent juries from hearing cases. He also argues that congressional support for tort reform laws further weakens the jury system. However, White concludes that the American people will ensure that the right to trial by jury will be preserved. White is an associate general counsel of the Association of Trial Lawyers of America.

As you read, consider the following questions:
1. How is the jury portrayed in the press, in White's opinion?
2. According to the author, how do federal judges act as "gatekeepers"?
3. Why does White believe people should be optimistic about the future of the American jury?

Excerpted from "The Civil Jury: 200 Years Under Siege," by Jeffrey Robert White, *Trial*, June 2000. Copyright © 2000 by Trial Magazine. Reprinted with permission.

A fine compliment to the Association of Trial Lawyers of America appeared in—of all places—the editorial page of the *Wall Street Journal*: "Over the years, [ATLA] has developed a reputation for success on Capitol Hill with a simple but powerful message that the right to a jury trial embedded in the Seventh Amendment should be preserved at all costs."

For over half a century, ATLA has devoted its efforts, talents, and resources to that mission. The text of the Seventh Amendment is inscribed on the front of ATLA's headquarters building in Washington, D.C.: "In suits at common law, where the value in controversy shall exceed twenty dollars, the right of trial by jury shall be preserved, and no fact tried by a jury, shall be otherwise reexamined in any court of the United States, than according to the rules of common law."

Legislative and Judicial Attacks

For much of the association's history, the civil jury has been under heavy assault. State legislatures have enacted hundreds of tort "reform" statutes to limit its authority, and Congress's repeated attempts to do the same have failed only narrowly.

Judges have become bolder in taking issues away from the jury—both before and after the verdict—and routinely remit damage awards. Federal preemption of state tort law, class action settlements, and mandatory arbitration—all pressed by corporate defendants and blessed by federal judges—threaten to take entire classes of cases out of the hands of juries. In the legal literature and the popular press, the jury is demeaned as incompetent, inefficient, and untrustworthy. Through it all, trial lawyers have insisted that the Seventh Amendment means what it says.

Wait, some may say. Doesn't this mission lack a certain loftiness? If the jury's purpose is, as the Supreme Court stated, merely "to assure a fair and equitable resolution of factual issues" in civil cases, what is to be lost by handing over this procedural task (which many citizens avoid if at all possible) to more competent and efficient judges, panels of experts, or professional arbitrators? In short, is the civil jury worth fighting for?

If the civil jury fades from the American civil justice system, it will be because its opponents have succeeded in marginalizing it as an antique fact detector, hardly worth manning the barricades to defend. . . .

Modern Attacks on Juries

The public relations campaign turned a good deal nastier in the mid-1980s and 1990s when it became part of an aggressive lobbying campaign for state and federal tort "reform." Its success in garnering public support came from skillful use of "crazy cases." Some anecdotes were simply gross distortions of the facts in a particular lawsuit, such as the portrayal of the McDonald's coffee case. Others, including the widely repeated story of the man lifting his lawnmower to trim his hedges, were completely fictitious.

The message pounded into the public consciousness, repeated in legislative hearings and in court briefs, was that juries are mindless and perverse, easily manipulated by greedy plaintiff lawyers (not a flattering reflection on well-paid defense counsel), and utterly lacking in common sense (not a flattering view of the American public from whose midst jurors are drawn).

Even greater than the harm to injury victims due to tort "reform" statutes is the damage to democratic values caused by this drumbeat of jury bashing.

The Supreme Court and the Jury System

Will the new century see a new defense of the civil jury?

Representatives in Congress and the state legislatures show few signs of willingness to say no to corporate contributors demanding greater protection from juries. The press, the direct beneficiary of the courageous juries in *Zenger*, *Wilkes*, and other cases, is frequently guided by its own business interests.

The Supreme Court has relied on the Seventh Amendment to turn aside some overt attempts to eliminate the jury entirely. Congress may not, in a move reminiscent of King George III of England, shift cases from Article III courts to jury-free Article I tribunals. Class action attorneys may not trade away the jury rights of any future asbestos victims in order to fashion a compensation scheme for numerous claimants.

Relying on the decisions in *Wilkes* and *Dimick*, the Supreme Court unanimously ruled that where a federal statute provides a cause of action analogous to a suit at common law, not only do parties have a right to a jury under the Seventh Amendment, but also "the right to a jury trial includes the right to have a jury determine the amount of statutory damages."

THE JURY SYSTEM   THE ALTERNATIVE

Conrad. © 1994 by Los Angeles Times Syndicate. Reprinted with permission.

On the other hand, the Court has not hesitated to expand the authority of federal judges to restrict juries. The Court found that the Seventh Amendment was no impediment to requiring federal judges to act as "gatekeepers" to exclude expert testimony they deem unreliable, requiring district courts in diversity suits to review federal jury awards under more stringent state tort "reform" provisions, and requiring even state courts to undertake review of punitive damages awards for possible excessiveness.

Following the High Court's lead, federal district courts and courts of appeals have become measurably more activist in using directed verdicts and summary judgments to prevent tort cases from reaching juries and in using remittitur to reduce jury awards.

Positive Developments

There have also been encouraging developments. State supreme courts have reinvigorated state constitutional guarantees, including the right to a remedy and the right to trial by jury, to invalidate tort "reform" legislation.

In addition, the overstated propaganda attacks on the civil jury have prompted researchers to conduct empirical studies of jury performance. The results have borne out the wisdom of the Seventh Amendment. In sharp contrast to the "crazy" juries lampooned in propagandists' anecdotes, these studies overwhelmingly have found that real juries perform their duties remarkably well.

Juries follow the court's instructions conscientiously and base their decisions on evidence rather than emotion. Their decisions are generally in line with what judges or professional arbitrators would have decided, demonstrating that juries are capable of doing justice in even complex cases. Nor are judges demonstrably better decisionmakers than juries are. Not only are judges and arbitrators drawn from a fairly narrow segment of American society, but also they are subject to a measurable bias toward the court system's "repeat players," who are, overwhelmingly, corporate defendants.

Legal scholars, who had virtually ignored the Seventh Amendment until 1966, have in recent decades enlivened analysis of the civil jury not as a mere rule of procedure but as an instrument of participatory democracy.

How to Save the Jury

Court decisions, empirical studies, and law review articles are not themselves likely to save the jury (as a century ago they were not sufficient to eliminate it). The right to trial by jury will be preserved in this new century, as before, by the American people themselves.

If history provides a guide, this right may be reinvigorated as part of a grassroots, populist-style movement pressing for broader changes. In the late 18th and early 20th centuries, those movements enflamed activists who identified with the great majority of working Americans, were alarmed at the power of commercial interests to influence the instruments of government and obtain special protections against accountability, and valued the direct participation of ordinary citizens in governing.

Certainly, the growing activism in favor of campaign finance reform could portend such a movement. So, too, does the growing importance of the inherently democratic Internet.

Perhaps the greatest reason for optimism is that in our history political truths eventually prevail. From the moment America accepted as self-evident the truth "that all men are created equal," slavery became a lie that was ultimately swept away. The broad attacks on the civil jury are premised on the most corrosive lie that can be told to a democratic society: that the people are incapable of governing. The jury surely needs to be improved, made more effective and even more efficient. And it will be preserved.

"Judicial opinion notwithstanding, the right of jury nullification stands timeless and irrevocable."

The Jury System Should Permit Nullification

Nathan Lapp

Jurors should be allowed to nullify laws they believe are unfair and acquit defendants who have violated such laws, Nathan Lapp contends in the following viewpoint. According to Lapp, the right to nullification has a long history, dating back to the acquittals of William Penn and John Peter Zenger. However, he argues, many modern-day judges are unwilling to acknowledge the right of jurors to judge the law. Lapp maintains that jury nullification must again become an accepted right because of the indispensable and important role of jurors. Lapp is a freelance writer and coordinator of the New York Fully Informed Jury Association, an organization that seeks to inform Americans about their rights and responsibilities when serving as trial jurors.

As you read, consider the following questions:

1. According to Lapp, why did Thomas Jefferson endorse trial by jury?
2. In the author's view, who were "the unsung heroes" of the John Peter Zenger case?
3. Why does Lapp believe that jurors have a unique influence in the evolution of law?

W hen disputes arise over who has the freedom to do what, fundamental principles of fairness, or "right reason," as Roman philosopher Cicero phrased it, must come into play. For this task, the founders recommended trial by jury.

A Historical Role

As George Mason stated in his Virginia Declaration of Rights (1776): "In controversies respecting property, and in suits between man and man, the ancient trial by jury is preferable to any other, and ought to be held sacred." Thomas Jefferson endorsed trial by jury as a damper on government, writing in a letter to Thomas Paine in 1789 that he considered trial by jury "the only anchor ever yet imagined by man, by which a government can be held to the principles of its constitution."

Fifteen years after Mason authored the Virginia Declaration of Rights, the U.S. Bill of Right's Seventh Amendment inherited Mason's original theme: ". . . where the value in controversy exceeds twenty dollars, the right of trial by jury shall be preserved. . . ." In other words, if even a seemingly insignificant portion of someone's liberty was disputed— whether by government or private individuals—trial by jury would be mandatory. The jury became a maintenance tool of freedom.

But today our juries are in trouble. In a passion to uphold law and order, America's legal institutions have almost forgotten the jury's role as protector of freedom. The jury is frequently tinkered with in ways that government planners consider progress. Prospective jurors may be graded for religious, philosophical, and personal beliefs. This involves a terribly inefficient selection process that yields juries sanitized to government specification, in lieu of the ancient, randomly chosen jury of peers. Once selected, jury members can be quarantined, gagged, and barred from taking notes or asking questions. Trial judges may suppress critical evidence or even conduct much of the proceedings in the jury's absence.

As an advocate of jury rights and a court watcher, I have observed the treatment of trial jurors. I find it remarkable that in a free country certain citizens not accused of any crime can be ordered about in such a cold, cavalier manner.

Like so many vassals, jurors resign their freedoms to the court—with only modest remuneration for their efforts.

Meanwhile, our state, federal, and administrative tribunals operate in a fashion that precludes all but a trifle of criminal cases even to be tried by jury. This is the form of due process that many Americans, especially judicial system insiders, seem to feel comfortable with.

Jurors Cannot Fulfill Their Duties

I believe there is reasonable doubt whether our jury system, thus regimented, can fulfill the purpose for which it was intended. In 1973, Supreme Court Justice William Douglas wrote: "It is indeed common knowledge that the grand jury, having been conceived as a bulwark between the citizen and the Government, is now a tool of the Executive." If the deterioration of the grand jury is any indicator of the subversion of due process in our courts, it stands to reason that our trial jury system is equally dysfunctional.

Perhaps the practice that most frequently undermines jurors is the mandate that they must render a verdict based exclusively on their finding of facts, with no consideration of the integrity of the law or its application. During the charge to the jury, jurors often hear a command of this sort from the bench: "You must take the law as I give it to you whether you agree with it or not. You are the sole judges of the facts, I am the sole Judge of the law."

Vogue as it may be, such instruction delivers a three-dimensional invasion into the province of the jury.

First, to forbid the jury to assess the law adulterates trial by jury as originally instituted. The founders—both in practice and in principles that formed early American governments—expressly endorsed the jury's role as judges of both law and fact. John Adams, in a statement prior to his election as the second president, was not in the least oblique regarding the jury's proper sphere: "It is not only . . . [the juror's] right, but his duty to find the verdict according to his own best understanding, judgement, and conscience, though in direct opposition to the direction of the court."

Second, the prohibition legalizes a double standard of justice. One set of rules exists for jurists, who may exercise veto power by dropping charges, dismissing cases, overruling previous court decisions, or using ordinary discretion in the execution of laws. Another set of rules is laid out for common citizens, the jurors. Hearing identical arguments in a case, the jurors must follow the rules imposed by the court, with no consideration for conscience or justice. Thus, a great chasm divides the ordinary citizen from the people outfitted with badges and gavels.

Third and most important, instructions that tell jurors they have no discretion when it comes to law are untrue and an encroachment upon the people's mind and conscience. To tell the jury that it does not have the right to consider the law in reaching its verdict is to stipulate that it may not mistrust the government. It is also to concede that commonsense appraisal of individual circumstances is not permitted without legislative consent.

The William Penn Case

Consider the dichotomy between contemporary jury instructions and those given during the first jury trial conducted by the Supreme Court of the United States: "But it must be observed that by the same law, which recognizes this reasonable distribution of jurisdiction (Judges as judges of law, jurors as judges of facts), you have, nevertheless, a right to take upon yourselves to judge of both, and to determine the law as well as the fact in controversy."

The function of trial juries was also defined by lexicographer Noah Webster in 1828: "[Petty juries], consisting usually of twelve men, attend courts to try matters of fact in civil causes, and to decide both the law and the fact in criminal prosecutions." Webster's observation solidifies the contention that jury latitude in applying the law was once axiomatic of trials by jury.

Webster did not invent the meaning of trial by jury. Jury power was tested 150 years earlier in England, when jurors refused to return a guilty verdict based on facts in the trial of William Penn. Penn's crime? Allegedly, disturbing the peace by publicly preaching the Quaker religion.

On August 31, 1670, William Penn was arrested and brought before the court at the Old Bailey in London. The jury heard from two constables and a sergeant who testified about Penn's preaching at a time when England's Conventicle Act forbade Quakerism as a form of worship. With all evidence pointing to Penn's defiance of the act, the court charged the jury, coaxing them to deliver a speedy verdict of guilty.

Jurors Are Not Incompetent

If jurors are not competent to judge the law, how could they be competent to vote for the legislators who write the laws, or the judges who interpret the laws, or the referenda or initiatives that are on the ballot in many states?

If we believe that jurors are not competent to judge the law after hearing every detail of the case, and after hearing the law and the facts argued and explained to them at great length, then we have to believe that judging the law is a significantly more difficult task than is required of voters, following whatever minimal investigation they have performed on their own. I do not believe that argument can be made with a straight face.

Clay S. Conrad, *FIJActivist*, Winter/Spring 1999.

When the jury returned, the foreman announced that they could find Penn guilty only of preaching, but not of causing tumult or committing any crime. This so incensed the ten presiding judges that one, Sir Samuel Starling, remanded them to the jury room without food, water, or accommodations "until they brought in a lawful verdict." Undaunted, these 12 defiant men repeatedly returned to reiterate their true verdict, while the court each time stipulated a verdict of guilty. The stalemate continued, with the Penn jury incarcerated under most ignominious conditions.

Ten weeks later England's highest court ruled that the penalties and detention imposed upon the jury were illegal. William Penn's acquittal was acknowledged, and the prisoners—Penn's jury—were vindicated. The high court stated that "the court has no power to superimpose its opinion over that of the jury," resulting in an historic and powerful precedent for jury rights.

The idea that juries have the right to nullify bad laws was underscored on numerous occasions following Penn's acquittal, but perhaps with most historical significance during the

1735 New York case of newspaper publisher John Peter Zenger. Zenger printed a series of articles containing scathing accusations against colonial Governor William Cosby. Although the attorney general failed on several attempts to have Zenger indicted by a grand jury, the governor's council proceeded to carry out a campaign against Zenger on its own, charging him with the crime of seditious libel.

Presiding at Zenger's trial, Chief Justice James Delancey instructed the jury that they should leave matters of law to the court. Defense attorney Andrew Hamilton, citing the case of William Penn, responded that such a rule "in effect renders Juries useless, to say no worse." Hamilton hailed the people's right to remonstrate against the oppressions and evil conduct of their governors by "exposing and opposing arbitrary power." Were this right denied, Hamilton said, "the next step may make them slaves."

The jury voted to acquit after brief deliberation.

John Peter Zenger's defiant position not only secured the freedom of press Americans enjoy to this day, it also helped annul the dubious crime of seditious libel. But the unsung heroes in the Zenger case remain the jurors who withstood the dictation of a corrupt government so that justice could prevail.

By trial and error, so to speak, the jury evolved from the status of a subservient entity of the English Crown to the independent body that eighteenth-century jurist William Blackstone would extol as a palladium of liberty. To this day, the state constitutions of Maryland, Indiana, and New York specifically honor jurors as "Judges of Law, as well as of fact."

Opposition by Judges

But today many judges despise the concept that made juries instrumental in freeing this country from the tyranny of witch hunts, slavery, and prohibition. In the case of *Wisconsin v. Leroy Reed*, subject of a 1995 PBS *Frontline* television documentary "Inside the Jury Room," the presiding judge declined to instruct jurors concerning their right to weigh the application of a law because "that would be an invitation to anarchy." (The defense counsel was permitted to argue to the jury that it had such a right.) A Rhode Island prosecutor recently told the grand jury in a criminal case: "We do not have jury nullification in Rhode Island."

In a report published in *The Judges' Journal* in 1996, Justice Frederic B. Rodgers of Gilpin County, Colorado, alluded to the danger of "runaway juries," recommending that courts monitor closely for evidence of nullification sentiment. Unrepentant nullifiers, he advised, should be excused from service.

Not all modern judges agree, however. In 1972, Chief Judge David Bazelon of the U.S. Court of Appeals for the District of Columbia acknowledged the jury's right to judge the law: "The pages of history shine on instances of the jury's exercise of its prerogative to disregard uncontradicted evidence and instructions of the judge." He cited the Zenger case and prosecutions of violators of the fugitive slave law. His opinion also quoted eminent legal scholar Roscoe Pound, who said in 1910, "Jury lawlessness is the greatest corrective of law in its actual administration."

Today this is a minority view. But judicial opinion notwithstanding, the right of jury nullification stands timeless and irrevocable. To doubt its existence is to embrace the myth that judges can acquire lordship of the jury's conscience. In fact, no government authority can steal the people's last check on laws haphazardly written—or good laws haphazardly enforced. Judges cannot proclaim a monopoly on the law—without aligning themselves with the likes of the ten judges who prosecuted William Penn. No prosecutor or judge can demand that a verdict be rendered exclusively on the jury's finding of fact, without trivializing the moral reasoning on which the Penn jury and many juries since then have stood firm.

Protecting Citizens from Problematic Laws

As responsible citizens, we ought to think about the consistency of written law. Laws are often byproducts of special-interest, legislative, and judicial power struggles. The desired result of law is to protect society from bullies, or as Thomas Jefferson said, "to restrain men from injuring one another." Unfortunately, every law, regardless of how well it works, can be turned to violate the rights of the people.

Take the case involving one-year-old Andrew Roberts, who was mauled by a wandering dog while waiting with his mother outside a California coffee shop. Andrew's father, after seeing what the dog had done to his son, located the Akita-Chow mix and dispatched him with a baseball bat.

Roberts claimed responsibility, and the state of California tried him for cruelty to animals. Roberts faced a year in prison, but a jury voted to acquit him.

The jury did not deny that it was cruel to bludgeon a dog with a baseball bat. They did not say that there should be no law against cruelty to animals. They did not assume the role of legislator and strike the law from the books. But they concluded that justice would not be served by applying the law to the case at hand. By nullifying the law, the Roberts jury actually helped make the animal cruelty law safer since future prosecutors would exercise caution before they used it to harass another citizen. The moral is that laws can be enforced in ways that the legislature or the citizen or even the judiciary never dreamed of. The jury, then, must ensure that justice is delivered whenever the naked force of written law would unduly threaten someone's freedom.

The late Harry Moss, Sr., a Ventura, California, attorney, once wrote in an essay: "Law, after all is merely a bunch of rules written by the legislature. Justice is based on the relationship between people and is certainly not just a bunch of rules. Anyone who cannot make this distinction should not be sitting on the bench." Moss illustrated that Germany had many fine judges—until Hitler took over and the horrors of the Nazi state became legal. Then, those same fine judges continued to enforce the law without observing that it had become unjust. Moss does not excuse them: "Justice requires that no law can require you to commit an unjust act."

The Jury Is the Law

Finally, we should remember that jury nullification no more flouts the rule of law than does jurist nullification or legislative repeal. The jury, by virtue of its commission and verdict, is the law. It is to the jury that we turn for help when human vices and weaknesses prevent us from resolving disputes privately. We implore the jury for justice, for mercy, for circumspection. We put lives and freedom in the hands of jurors. Their influence on the evolution of law is unique because they evaluate its impact firsthand, rather than from the comfortable vantage point of the bench, the legislative chamber, academia, or lobbying outfit. They see and touch the law as applied to fellow human beings and, hence, to themselves.

The championing of jury rights does, however, accompany the sobering realization that jury power can be abused. Jury decisions are only as perfect as the cross section of people it comprises, and if the overall character of a citizenry is deficient, a departure from justice in our courtrooms may certainly follow. But the restoration of American juries to the position they had in times past is unlikely to produce a power as dangerous as the one currently vested in the high places of government.

George Mason wrote in his Declaration of Rights that the blessings of liberty "cannot be preserved to any people but by firm adherence to justice, moderation, temperance, frugality, virtue, and by frequent recurrence to fundamental principles." Let the institution of trial by jury once again serve as a vehicle for those principles. Let the men and women to whom we delegate the scales of justice be respected for their indispensable role as guardians of liberty.

*"It is not feasible to try to separate 'good'
nullification from 'bad.'"*

Jury Nullification Is Unfair

Nancy King

Jury nullification should be prohibited for several reasons,
Nancy King argues in the following viewpoint. She argues
that while nullification has sometimes been used as a weapon
against oppressive laws, it has also been a means to acquit
people who committed crimes against African Americans
and to acquit rapists if the jury believed the victim dressed or
acted provocatively. She also disputes the assertion that jurors are more qualified than legislators in determining
whether a law is just. King concludes that judges must take
steps to ensure that juries are not prevented from delivering
an appropriate verdict because of the political views and personal opinions of one or two jurors. King is an associate dean
and professor at Vanderbilt University Law School in
Nashville, Tennessee.

As you read, consider the following questions:
1. According to King, why was the Klan Act passed?
2. Why does King think that jurors are not qualified to
   decide whether or not a law is just?
3. What steps does the author suggest judges should take
   to prevent nullification?

From "No: Don't Give Society's Mavericks Another Tool to Subvert the Will of
the People," by Nancy King, *Insight on the News*, May 24, 1999. Copyright © 1999
by *Insight on the News*. Reprinted with permission.

Inviting jurors to acquit regardless of what the law says is a tempting cure-all for the law's ills. But cultivating jury nullification is a mistake. Like the peddler's elixir, jury nullification is just as likely to produce unpleasant side effects as it is to bring relief. The most compelling reasons to be wary of the practice of jury nullification are the very arguments its advocates trot out in its defense—history, democracy, fairness, political change and the Constitution itself.

The Dangers of Nullification

One does not have to look back far into history to find a good reason for discouraging jury nullification. True, the colonists embraced the jury's power as a weapon against the king's oppressive laws. And, we're reminded, juries bravely blocked prosecutions of those who resisted the Fugitive Slave Act, Prohibition and the Vietnam War draft. But jury nullification has not been neatly confined to the rejection of "bad" law or the release of "good" defendants. A much less appealing pattern of jury lawlessness is also prominent in our nation's history. For generations juries have refused to convict or punish those who clearly are guilty of violence against unpopular victims, particularly African-Americans. The Klan Act, barring Ku Klux Klan sympathizers from juries after the Civil War, was passed because juries were exercising their "independence" to ignore civil-rights statutes. In Texas after the Civil War, prosecutors had to strike from juries those who "believe, morally, socially, politically, or religiously, that it is not murder for a white man to take the life of a [N]egro with malice aforethought." This is not a proud legacy. We should not assume that refusal to punish those who harm members of less popular groups is entirely behind us just because some juries, in some places, are more racially diverse than they used to be.

Racism, of course, is not the only risk. To invite nullification is to invite jurors to devise their own defenses to a criminal charge. All three branches of government may have labored to eliminate similar considerations from the assessment of guilt. Juries have acquitted defendants in rape cases after concluding that the victims deserved to be raped because of the way they dressed or acted. Jurors may acquit protesters who trespass, damage property or harm others if they conclude the defendants were right to bypass lawful means of redress. Jurors may believe that reasonable doubt is not a strong-enough burden of proof and require fingerprints or eyewitnesses before convicting. They may decide that certain conduct by the police should be a complete defense, oblivious of efforts by legislators and judges to craft remedies and regulations for police misconduct. Now, as in the past, encouraging "good" nullification inevitably means encouraging "bad" nullification as well, because there is no way to second-guess a jury's acquittal once delivered.

It is not feasible to try to separate "good" nullification from "bad." Even nullification advocates cannot agree on what type of nullification is acceptable. One supporter would require nullification instructions only in cases involving nonviolent acts of civil disobedience where the defendant had "given serious thought" to legal means of accomplishing the same objective. Another would encourage jury pronouncements on the law only when the issue was the constitutionality of a criminal statute. A third insists that "true" nullification is limited to decisions "based on conscientious grounds." In a survey, college students were asked whether jury nullification included any combination of a set of possible reasons for acquittal, all of which the researchers believed were valid reasons for juries to nullify, such as, "The police wrongfully assaulted the defendant after he was arrested." When only 13 percent of those surveyed agreed that nullification included all of the reasons listed, the researchers concluded their subjects had a lot to learn about nullification. The response should suggest something else—that it is wishful thinking to assume that legislators or judges will be able to agree when jurors should ignore the law and when they should not.

Not Equipped to Evaluate Laws

One might support expanding the lawmaking role of the jury if one believes juries are an essential feature of our democracy, better at assessing whether a law is "just" or "unjust" than democratically elected legislators. But juries probably are much worse at this task. Unlike legislators or electors, jurors have no opportunity to investigate or research the merits of legislation. Carefully stripped of those who know anything about the type of case or conduct at stake, juries are insulated from the information they would need to make reliable judgments about the costs and benefits, the justice or the injustices, of a particular criminal prohibition. Nor can jurors seek out information during the case. The so-called "safety valve" of jury nullification, which exempts a defendant here and there from the reach of a controversial law, actually reduces the pressure for those opposed to a truly flawed statute to lobby for its repeal or amendment and deprives appellate courts of opportunities to declare its flaws.

Nullification's supporters point out that legislatures cannot anticipate unfair applications of the laws they enact, so jury nullification is needed for "fine-tuning." But jurors are not in any better position than judges or prosecutors to decide which defendants should be exempted from a law's reach. Again, jurors probably are much worse at this function because they lack critical information. Any juror who actually knows the defendant is excused from the jury. Jurors only can speculate on the penalty that would follow from their verdict. Unless the defendant testifies (and most defendants do not), the jury will never hear him explain his side of the story nor learn whether he has a prior record. They may never learn of evidence suppressed because it was illegally obtained or because of other errors on the part of the prosecution. More importantly, because jurors decide only one case, they cannot compare the culpability of different defendants or assess the relative importance of enforcing a particular prohibition against a particular defendant. No doubt about it: Juries are excellent fact finders and lie detectors. But when facts are not in issue and guilt is clear, the ability of jurors to reach sound decisions about when the law should be suspended and when it should be applied is questionable at best.

Juries Should Not Be Political Tools

Jury nullification sometimes is touted as an effective political tool for those who have failed at the voting booth and on the legislative floor. There are two problems with this argument. First, if a group is not influential enough to obtain favorable legislation, it is not likely to secure a majority in the jury box. At most, jurors with dissenting views succeed in hanging the jury. But hung juries are a political dead end. The defendant is not spared; he can be tried again and convicted. More importantly, as a recent recommendation in California demonstrates, rising hung-jury rates inevitably lead to proposals to eliminate the unanimity requirement, proposals that if adopted would shut down minority viewpoints more effectively than any instruction against nullification ever could.

Responding to Pro-Nullification Arguments

While many adherents of jury nullification acknowledge certain past limitations of the practice—such as the unwillingness of Southern white juries to convict Caucasians of killing African-Americans or Jews—they believe that juries should be allowed to act as they wish. A brief rundown on their arguments and our response follows.

1. Laws are often unfair or unjust.

We don't disagree with that statement. But we question the advisability of leaving laws to idiosyncratic evaluation, where an individual's personal feeling about justice and fairness determines whether an acquittal or conviction should result. Doesn't this potentially imply a denial of responsibility for any of our actions? Aren't the laws based upon what the majority has decided? Do we really want a system where there is no equal justice for all?

2. Jurors who are determined to nullify will do so.

We can't prevent juries from rendering a crude justice but we don't have to encourage vigilante rule.

3. Juries are the conscience of the community.

Who appointed them? Not those who wrote the U.S. Constitution. In fact, many analysts would say that juries are a peculiar minority of the community consisting of the under- or unemployed, tending to be people with little education, who don't read the newspapers or watch or listen to the news. They are young, elderly, and they are disproportionately white.

Laurence H. Gellen and Peter Hemenway, *Last Chance for Justice*, 1997.

Even if a politically unsuccessful group finds strength in some local jury boxes, should we really be heartened by the prospect of being stuck with the decision of 12 people who have been encouraged to ignore the pronouncements of the state or nation's elected representatives? If there is a concentrated population of homophobes, racists or anti-Semites in my state, I, for one, do not want judges and lawyers encouraging jurors drawn from these communities to apply their own standards—standards that may vary with the victim's sexual orientation, race or religion. Local dissent, of course, is not limited to group-based views. People disagree strongly about a variety of laws—laws against possessing weapons, euthanasia, driving after a couple of drinks, the use of marijuana, slapping one's wife or children around or the dumping of paint or oil. There are places well-suited for resolving these disagreements: the legislature and the polling booth. Our democratic process should not be jettisoned arbitrarily by an unelected group of citizens who need never explain themselves.

Finally, the Constitution does not support an enhanced lawmaking role for juries. Jurors have no personal constitutional right to disregard the law—otherwise, they would not be required to take an oath to obey it. Nor do defendants have a constitutional right to insist that jurors be given the opportunity to disregard the law. True, judges cannot overturn a conviction or acquittal without the consent of the defendant (through appeal, motion or otherwise). But this rule is in place not because the Constitution considers the jury a superior lawmaker but because the Fifth Amendment prohibits the government from putting the defendant in jeopardy of life or limb more than once for the same offense. Judges also are barred from directing verdicts of guilt, but only because the Sixth Amendment guarantees to the defendant a jury's assessment of the facts.

Preventing Nullification

Beyond what is necessary to protect these important interests of the accused, our refusal to tolerate jury nullification must not stray. Judges, for example, should continue to avoid seating jurors who cannot or will not promise to follow the judge's instructions; continue to prohibit argument and deny instructions concerning defenses not supported by the evidence; continue to instruct jurors about the law and require them to follow these instructions; and continue to prohibit nullification advocates from approaching jurors with nullification propaganda (just as they bar prosecution sympathizers from lobbying the jury for conviction). Although each of these practices is designed to prevent jury nullification, each is constitutional because the Constitution does not protect jury nullification itself. It protects a defendant's right to fact-finding by a jury and to the finality of a verdict.

Legislators and judges so far steadfastly have rejected repeated proposals to lower barriers to jury nullification because they understand that the costs of such changes would far outweigh any benefits they may bring. Other fundamental changes in our jury system, such as the Supreme Court's decision to ban race-based peremptory challenges as a violation of the equal-protection rights of potential jurors, have been preceded by sustained social, political and legal critique of the status quo. A similar groundswell to cede more power to those who sit in jury boxes in criminal cases has never existed and, fortunately, probably never will.

| *"The peremptory challenge is essential to protecting the rights of litigants."*

Peremptory Challenges Are Necessary

Bobby Lee Cook and Michael A. Sullivan

In the following viewpoint, Bobby Lee Cook and Michael A. Sullivan maintain that peremptory challenges should not be eliminated. They argue that these challenges, which enable lawyers to prevent potential jurors from serving on a trial, have a long and well-established history. According to the authors, it is unlikely that the most biased people could be kept from jury service if such challenges are eliminated. They assert that peremptory challenges ensure that the jurors who are seated will judge a case based on evidence instead of personal biases and guarantee that trials remain fair in both appearance and fact. Cook is a criminal defense attorney, and Sullivan is a trial lawyer.

As you read, consider the following questions:

1. In what year did Roman law permit peremptory challenges, as stated by the authors?
2. Why do Cook and Sullivan say "peremptories provide a safety net"?
3. According to the authors, what would be the costs if peremptory challenges are eliminated?

R azing landmarks usually provokes justifiable outrage. So should recent proposals to take a wrecking ball to an enduring landmark of the judicial process—peremptory challenges.

A Long History

Over two thousand years, peremptory challenges have become a mainstay of our common law tradition. Roman law provided for peremptory challenges by statute as early as 104 B.C. Centuries later, [William] Blackstone memorialized the peremptory challenge as "a provision full of that tenderness and humanity to prisoners, for which the English laws are justly famous."

In the United States, Congress in 1790 embraced this tradition in capital cases. Since then, peremptory challenges have become firmly rooted in federal and state jury trials, both civil and criminal.

Although critics now deem this institution unnecessary, the Supreme Court in 1893 described the peremptory challenge as "one of the most important rights secured to the accused." More than once the Court has declared it per se, reversible error to impair the use of peremptory challenges, even though the Constitution does not require them.

The Benefits of Peremptories

Just as in Blackstone's time, potential jurors differ in their biases. As human beings, they also differ in their willingness and ability to be responsible and fair. It is fantasy to believe that, without peremptories, our standards for eliminating jurors for "cause" will keep the most biased, the least responsible, and the least fair persons from jury service. Even Justice [Antonin] Scalia has observed that "there really is no substitute for the peremptory. Voir dire . . . cannot fill the gap. The biases that go along with group characteristics tend to be biases that the juror himself does not perceive, so that it is no use asking about them."

Peremptories provide a safety net. They allow each side to exclude a few potential jurors who, based on "sudden impressions," facial expressions, body language, intuition, and the like, one side perceives are probably the most biased in favor of the other side. The remaining jurors, judged by the parties themselves as likely the least biased, decide the case. The parties' involvement is critical to the appearance of fairness, especially in criminal cases.

Prosecutors, for example, sometimes strike potential jurors whose family members have had negative experiences with law enforcement, even if the jurors do not admit actual bias. Because each jury venire is unique, the prosecutor may not have enough peremptory challenges to strike all such prospective jurors, but some strikes are preferable to none. In addition, peremptories help solve the problem that voir dire creates—that the "bare questioning [of a juror's] indifference may sometimes provoke a resentment." With the "extremes" of apparent partiality eliminated, both the appearance and reality of fairness are served.

The Supreme Court has pointed out still other virtues of peremptory challenges: The function of the challenge is not only to eliminate extremes of partiality on both sides, but to assure the parties that the jurors before whom they try the case will decide on the basis of the evidence placed before them, and not otherwise. In this way, the peremptory satisfies the rule that "to perform its high function in the best way 'justice must satisfy the appearance of justice.'"

Why Criticism of Peremptories Is Wrong

Critics of peremptories ask us to use less care in jury selection than in our everyday affairs. Consider how we routinely make other decisions that are no more demanding than whether to take away life or liberty. In hiring employees or child care providers, for example, would we ever agree to hire the first candidate who met our minimum objective standards? Or would we wish to interview several candidates, get a sense of each one as a person, and trust our gut feelings about potential problems that may nonetheless be difficult to articulate?

In many contexts, we regularly make these decisions based not on impermissible discrimination, but on objective criteria and our subjective sense of whether this person will be responsible and fair. Eliminating or restricting that same process in jury selection would create a double standard that would undercut confidence in, and trivialize, the fairness of the judicial system.

Getting to Know the Jury

I do not want a jury of blacks to judge my black defendant. I want a jury who likes me, is going to like him and then render a verdict of not guilty at the end. Therefore, if you let me know more about those assembled individuals, about their kids and their grandparents, about their ideas, feelings, thoughts and nuances, then I am less likely to stereotype them as women, blacks or other labels with which we work, which have some basis in reality, but in practice distort our perceptions. As a defense attorney, I can begin to focus on real things, on real feelings about the nature of the trial, and then begin to participate in the process that may have a racial element and a gender component.

For example, one of the experiences I have had in twenty years of trying cases is that women are stronger than men. If I have a choice between women jurors who I think will go my way and men, I want the women. My experience has been that almost every hung jury I have had involved one or two women, usually of good size, who sat in the corner, folded their arms and said, "I am not convicting this defendant." I cannot explain those dynamics. Women are superior to men in many contexts and so I want to make gender-based decisions. The fact of the matter is that gender and race and all of these things we pretend to eschew lie at the heart of all of the political and social decisions we make in our lives.

Raymond Brown, *American Criminal Law Review*, 1994.

What has changed over two millennia to warrant these recent attacks on peremptories? Human nature certainly has not, and peremptories remain essential to fulfill all of their historical purposes.

The only apparent change is the Supreme Court's Batson decision, which banned race discrimination by prosecutors in peremptory strikes. After Batson, Talladega County, Alabama, for example, would find it difficult to continue to exclude all black citizens from jury service, both through selection of the venire and use of peremptory strikes. The Batson doctrine has now spread to cover civil litigants, criminal defendants, and classifications other than race. There is no reason, however, to abandon the peremptory simply because of the Batson requirements, and rules for ensuring harmony between the peremptory and Batson have already been formulated.

Peremptories Are Not Misused

Other rationales for limiting peremptories are just as elusive and flawed. There is no evidence of an increase in misuse of peremptories; with scrutiny under Batson, the opposite is more likely. Nor is there any evidence, statistical or otherwise, that parties enjoy too many peremptory strikes, or that fewer strikes would be adequate to eliminate biased jurors. Every trial lawyer has seen the reverse prove true.

Concerns for infringing the rights of stricken jurors by use of "stereotypes" often overlook that the parties have the most at stake in a trial, and few if any potential jurors are clamoring to serve. Those concerns also ignore the true incentive of the lawyer in using peremptory strikes. The attorney risks losing if he does not look beyond stereotypes for actual signs of bias, unfairness, or irresponsibility among potential jurors.

When critics complain that peremptories interfere with having a fair cross-section of the community represented on the jury, they ignore that the Sixth Amendment's fair cross-section requirement concerns the venire from which the jury is selected, and not the petit jury itself. Most telling, however, the critics say little, if anything, about meaningful steps to broaden the venire. Do these critics, for example, also call for canvassing homeless shelters to create a more representative venire from which the jury may be drawn?

An Essential Landmark

The critics also must recognize that eliminating the screening function of peremptories would have a heavy cost. Lengthier and more probing voir dire would be necessary to ferret out actual bias among potential jurors, followed by legal argument over whether these potential jurors should be excused for "cause."

The more likely outcome—impliedly preferred by those who claim eliminating peremptories will "speed up" trials—is that this screening of potentially biased or unfair jurors will go undone. Questionable candidates with personal agendas may give "correct" answers to voir dire questions, escape challenge for "cause," and take seats in the jury box to sit in judgment. Peremptories may not have excluded all such persons, but at least would have given the parties a chance to try. With peremptories eliminated or reduced, the trial process would become less reliable and less fair, both in appearance and in fact.

As those prosecutors, criminal defense lawyers, and civil lawyers who actually try cases usually agree, the peremptory challenge is essential to protecting the rights of litigants. It is a landmark worth preserving.

> *"Litigants are being permitted to eliminate competent individuals from juries for reasons that need not rise to the level of a strike for good cause."*

Peremptory Challenges Are Unfair

Gregory E. Mize

In the following viewpoint, Gregory E. Mize asserts that peremptory challenges are unfair because they prevent competent people from serving on juries. According to Mize, peremptory challenges lead to gender and racial profiling. Mize cites an experience he had with a rejected juror who questioned why such challenges led to an all-female, primarily African American, jury. Mize concludes that policy makers need to consider the effects of this legal tool. Mize is an associate judge of the District of Columbia Superior Court.

As you read, consider the following questions:
1. What does "for cause" mean, as defined by Mize?
2. According to the rejected juror, what assumption does the justice system need to get past?
3. According to Mize, how many peremptory challenges do both sides receive?

From "A Legal Discrimination," by Gregory E. Mize, *The Washington Post*, October 8, 2000. Copyright © 2000 by Washington Post Writers Group. Reprinted by permission of the author.

O n a typical Monday morning, a group of D.C. residents—beautifully reflective of our community in terms of gender, race and ethnicity—came to my courtroom for jury selection in a personal injury case.

They listened to my pep talk about the virtues of jury service and about the importance of their oath to tell the truth during the selection interviews. I told them that the purpose of the questioning was to learn if anything in their experience would stand in the way of their being fair in the case.

Eliminating Jurors

It took about 45 minutes for the group to be questioned, collectively and then individually, by the lawyers and by myself, to ferret out any grounds to excuse someone "for cause"—legalese meaning a juror likely would not be impartial.

After I ruled on motions by the lawyers to strike a citizen for cause, there came the centuries-old legal procedure called peremptory challenge, during which a party can strike a citizen from service based on hunch, instinct, social "science" or whatever.

Accordingly, each side exercised the three peremptories provided it by law. The plaintiff (an African American man) struck three white men, and the defendant (a corporation) struck two white males and one African American female. Relying on doctrine from the Supreme Court, I called upon the plaintiff's attorney to provide the reasons for his apparent gender- and race-oriented use of peremptory strikes. The counsel gave various non-gender and non-race-based rationales for his actions. By law, I had to honor his strikes. As a result, an all-female jury of five African Americans and two whites was seated.

One Man's Reaction

Before the trial began, one of those rejected, a middle-aged white man, returned to the courtroom and asked to speak to me. The court reporter recorded his words.

"With all due respect to everyone involved in the proceedings," he said, "I have a concern based upon what I understood was your guidance and your telling us the criteria that are used for jury selection. If I understood you correctly, you said race and gender should not be used as selection criteria. It doesn't take a rocket scientist to realize that both gender and race were an issue in the selection of this jury. It was unmistakable to me and, I'm sure, to everyone else here."

He then added a haunting plea, "I want you all to look inside yourselves . . . to consider what the implications of this are for impartial justice."

Neither Fair nor Fundamental

No one has recently written more thoroughly or compellingly of the need to eliminate peremptory challenges than Judge Morris Hoffman, a state trial judge in Denver, Colorado.

In *Peremptory Challenges Should Be Abolished: A Trial Judge's Perspective*, 64 U. Chi. L. Rev. 809 (1997), Hoffman carefully traces the history of the peremptory challenge and demonstrates that it is not rooted in principles of fairness, impartiality, or protection of the rights of the accused; rather, it stems from "the now meaningless and quite undemocratic concept of royal infallibility," having been "invented two hundred years before the notion of jury impartiality" was conceived.

He also observes that "the Supreme Court has consistently and unflinchingly held that the peremptory challenge is neither a constitutionally necessary component of a defendant's right to an impartial jury, nor even so fundamental as to be part of federal common law."

Thomas F. Hogan, Gregory E. Mize, and Kathleen Clark, *World & I*, July 1998.

I told him that my own perceptions coincided with his and about my earlier challenges to one of the lawyers in that regard. This John Q. Citizen thanked me. "It is some consolation," he said of my explanation. . . . "[But] I think we need to get beyond the assumption that race and gender discrimination only work in the conventional historic directions. . . . That does little to further real justice and real race and gender equity in this country."

Profiling Is Taking Place

He then quietly left the courtroom. The trial proceeded smoothly to conclusion thereafter, but his words still resonate. He experienced a process in which he and his peers were asked many personal questions with the assurance that they were geared toward obtaining a truly fair and impartial jury. They were informed that the U.S. Supreme Court had outlawed anyone's being struck from jury duty merely because of race, gender or ethnicity. He and others were not challenged "for cause" by any of the parties. And yet, with the dash of a lawyer's pen, they were dismissed.

Many of us on the bench have seen this legal chess game during jury selection. Everyone is saying gender and race should not matter, but gender and racial profiling are being undertaken in the exercise of these largely hidden strikes. Litigants are being permitted to eliminate competent individuals from juries for reasons that need not rise to the level of a strike for good cause.

In felony criminal cases in federal and many state courts, this litigation weapon power is increased more than threefold, the government and the defendant each having—and almost always using—10 peremptories.

A Change Is Needed

Are peremptory strikes a reasonable means to produce impartial juries, which is what the Constitution mandates? Or are they really suited to creating the opposite? What if in the November elections candidates and their campaign teams similarly could sweep any of us out of the voting booth merely on the basis of complexion, grooming, facial expression or who knows what?

What kind of message do these attorney-client tools of intuition and suspicion send to our community? Should we not rely on strikes for good cause as the more relied upon means to eliminate citizens from trial service?

For the numerous citizens whose right to vote in the jury deliberation room is nullified by the veiled exercise of peremptory strikes, answers to those questions likely would encourage a policy change. Perhaps change will occur if policymakers show up for jury duty soon.

Periodical Bibliography

The following articles have been selected to supplement the diverse views presented in this chapter.

William F. Buckley Jr.   "Any Prospect for Jury Reform?" *National Review*, May 5, 1997.

D. Graham Burnett   "Anatomy of a Verdict," *New York Times Magazine*, August 26, 2001.

Clay S. Conrad   "Are Juries Competent to Judge the Law?" *FIJActivist*, Winter/Spring 1999.

B. Michael Dann,   "Waking Up Jurors, Shaking Up Courts," *Trial*,
interviewed by   July 1997.
Donald Dilworth

Ken Hamblin   "A Case Against Jury Nullification," *Conservative Chronicle*, June 11, 1997.

Jeff Herman   "Ending the U.S. Jury System Circus," *USA Today Magazine*, September 1997.

Thomas F. Hogan,   "How to Improve the Jury System," *World & I*,
Gregory E. Mize,   July 1998.
and Kathleen Clark

James Kilpatrick   "Jury Nullification Is Terrible Mischief," *Conservative Chronicle*, July 9, 1997.

Diane Leininger   "Power of 12," *ABA Journal*, August 2001.

Geoffrey Norman   "Juror Furor," *American Spectator*, March 1998.

Vin Suprynowicz   "Jury Trials Too Costly . . . or Just Too Hard to Control?" *FIJActivist*, Winter/Spring 1999.

Jeffrey Robert White   "The Civil Jury: 200 Years Under Siege," *Trial*, June 2000.

CHAPTER 3

Is the Criminal Justice System Fair?

Chapter Preface

In August 2001, prompted by concerns that indigent defendants in Coweta County, Georgia, were not receiving adequate legal representation, the Southern Center for Human Rights filed a class action suit against the county. The center asserts that "*Over half* of the poor people found guilty of some offense in the Superior Court of Coweta County in the last two and a half years *were not represented by counsel*." In addition, those defendants who did receive counsel "are processed through the system without essential components of effective representation such as adequate, private and confidential consultation with an attorney."

The situation in Coweta County arose despite the 1963 case *Gideon v. Wainwright*, in which the U.S. Supreme Court declared that an attorney must be provided to any defendant too poor to hire his or her own lawyer. While this mandate was intended to ensure that all Americans would receive adequate representation in criminal trials, many indigent defendants find themselves turning to lawyers who spend little time advocating for their clients.

Many of these lawyers are contract defenders. Under that system, attorneys and law firms bid for the right to represent a county's indigent defendants. Coweta County has two such contracts. The Southern Center asserts that because of excessive caseloads and a lack of staff and resources (which should have been provided by the county), those two lawyers do not effectively represent their clients. Most of the cases are resolved with guilty pleas instead of being brought to trial. However, Coweta County is not alone in that regard. In an article for the *American Prospect*, Alan Berlow cites a contract defender in another Georgia county who, out of 276 cases between 1993 and 1995, entered 262 guilty pleas.

Several solutions have been suggested to ensure that the rights set forth in *Gideon* are not ignored. The American Bar Association and the Department of Justice have launched a project to encourage states to establish indigent defense oversight commissions. Georgia is among the states with these commissions. In a study for the conservative think tank Heritage Foundation, Kenneth F. Boehm and Peter T. Flaherty—

the chairman and president, respectively, of the National Legal and Policy Center—contend that indigent representation can be improved by making it easier for poor defendants to hire private attorneys. They suggest that a federal income tax deduction will encourage pro bono work. Boehm and Flaherty also note that arbitration and meditation can be used to resolve minor criminal matters.

Although everyone is supposed to be treated fairly in the American legal system, the lawsuit in Coweta County suggests that does not always happen. In the following chapter, the authors debate the fairness of the justice system.

*"Widespread ['driving while black']
practices deeply undermine the
legitimacy—and, therefore, the
effectiveness—of the criminal justice
system."*

Racial Profiling Reduces the Effectiveness of the Criminal Justice System

David A. Harris

Racial profiling, including race-based traffic stops, under-mines the effectiveness and legitimacy of the criminal justice system, David A. Harris contends in the following viewpoint. He argues that these traffic stops—which are used as a pretext to search cars for drugs—causes the affected drivers to distrust the police and can ultimately make police work harder and more dangerous. Harris asserts that federal and state governments need to take steps to end racially motivated traffic stops. Harris is a professor at the University of Toledo College of Law in Toledo, Ohio.

As you read, consider the following questions:
1. According to Harris, how have African Americans and Latinos altered their driving habits?
2. In 1997, what percentage of cars stopped by California Highway Patrol canine units contained drugs?
3. What steps does Harris think the fifty largest American cities should take to reduce race-related traffic stops?

"When I see cops today, I don't feel like I'm protected. I'm thinking, 'Oh shoot, are they gonna pull me over, are they gonna stop me?' That's my reaction. I do not feel safe around cops."

—Emmanuel, early 30s, financial services executive

Race-based traffic stops turn one of the most ordinary and quintessentially American activities into an experience fraught with danger and risk for people of color. Because traffic stops can happen anywhere and anytime, millions of African Americans and Latinos alter their driving habits in ways that would never occur to most white Americans. Some completely avoid places like all-white suburbs, where they fear police harassment for looking "out of place." Some intentionally drive only bland cars or change the way they dress. Others who drive long distances even factor in extra time for the traffic stops that seem inevitable.

Surviving Traffic Stops

Perhaps the personal cost exacted by racially-biased traffic stops is clearest in the instructions given by minority parents to their children on how to behave if they are stopped by police, regardless of economic background or geographic region. African American parents know that traffic stops can lead to physical, even deadly, confrontations. Karen, a social worker, says that when her young son begins to drive, she knows what she'll tell him:

> The police are supposed to be there to protect and to serve, but you being black and being male, you've got two strikes against you. Keep your hands on the steering wheel, and do not run, because they will shoot you in your back. Let them do whatever they want to do. I know it's humiliating, but let them do whatever they want to do to make sure you get out of that situation alive. Deal with your emotions later. Your emotions are going to come second—or last.

Christopher Darden, the African American prosecutor in the O.J. Simpson case, says that to survive traffic stops, he "learned the rules of the game years before. . . . Don't move. Don't turn around. Don't give some rookie an excuse to shoot you." The perspective of Mr. Darden—who spent 14 years working closely with police to prosecute accused criminals—is not unique. And for people of color, it continues to be reinforced by far too many real-life experiences.

The Effects on the Criminal Justice System

Widespread "driving while black" (DWB) practices deeply undermine the legitimacy—and, therefore, the effectiveness—of the criminal justice system. Pretextual traffic stops fuel the belief that the police are not only unfair and biased, but untruthful as well. Each pretextual traffic stop involves an untruth, and both the officer and the driver recognize this. The alleged traffic infraction is not the real reason that the officer has stopped the driver. This becomes obvious when the officer asks the driver whether he or she is carrying drugs or guns and seeks consent to search the car. If the stop was really about enforcement of the traffic code, there would be no need for a search. Stopping a driver for a traffic offense when the officer's real purpose is drug interdiction is a lie—a legally sanctioned one, to be sure, but a lie nonetheless.

What happens when law enforcement embraces a tactic that is based on the systematic and transparent deception of overwhelmingly innocent people? And, what happens when that tactic is employed primarily against people of color? It should surprise no one that those who are the victims of police discrimination regard the testimony and statements of police with suspicion. If jurors don't believe truthful police testimony, crimes are left unpunished, law enforcement becomes much less effective, and the very people who need the police most are left less protected.

Pretext stops capture some who are guilty but at an unacceptably high societal cost. The practice undermines public confidence in law enforcement, erodes the legitimacy of the criminal justice system, and makes police work that much more difficult and dangerous.

Putting an End to Racial Profiling

Although this decades-old problem cannot be solved overnight, it is time to launch an all-out frontal assault on DWB. The American Civil Liberties Union [ACLU] calls on the U.S. Justice Department, law enforcement officials and state

105

and federal legislators to join us in a comprehensive, five-part battle plan against the scourge of racial profiling.

FIRST: End the use of pretext stops.

Virtually all of the thousands of complaints received by the ACLU about DWB—and every recent case and scandal in this area—seem to involve the use of traffic stops for non-traffic purposes, usually drug interdiction. Although the U.S. Supreme Court failed to declare searches subsequent to a pretextual stop unconstitutional, that does not mean that such a tactic is wise or effective from a law enforcement perspective.

An Invitation to Racial Profiling

The Supreme Court has all but invited racial profiling. In 1996 the Court upheld the practice of "pretextual traffic stops," in which police officers use the excuse of a traffic violation to stop motorists when they are investigating some other crime. The same year, the Court allowed the police to use the coercive setting of a traffic stop to obtain consent to search. Together, these rules allow the police to stop and search whomever they please on the roads, without having to demonstrate probable cause. And where the police are freed from the need to justify their actions, they appear to fall back on racial stereotypes. In Maryland, for example, blacks were 70 percent of those stopped and searched by Maryland State Police from January 1995 through December 1997, on a road where 17.5 percent of the drivers and speeders were black. New Jersey reported that 77 percent of those stopped and searched on its highways were black or Hispanic, even though only 13.5 percent of the drivers were black or Hispanic.

David Cole, *Nation*, October 11, 1999.

It is time for law enforcement professionals to use their own best professional judgment in scrutinizing the wisdom of the pretextual stop tactic. All the evidence to date suggests that using traffic laws for non-traffic purposes has been a disaster for people of color and has deeply eroded public confidence in law enforcement. Using minor traffic violations to find drugs on the highways is like asking officers to find needles in a haystack. In 1997 California Highway Patrol canine units stopped nearly 34,000 vehicles. Only two percent of them were carrying drugs. Law enforcement decisions based on hunches rather than evidence are going to suffer from racial stereotyping, whether conscious or unconscious.

Legislation Is Required

SECOND: Pass the Traffic Stops Statistics Study Act.

At the beginning of the 105th Congress, Rep. John Conyers (D-MI) introduced H.R. 118, the Traffic Stops Statistics Act, requiring the collection of several categories of data on each traffic stop, including the race of the driver and whether a search was performed. The Attorney General would then conduct a study analyzing the data. This would be the first nationwide, statistically rigorous study of these practices. The idea behind the bill was that if the study confirmed what people of color have experienced for years, it would put to rest the idea that African Americans and other people of color are exaggerating isolated anecdotes into a social problem. Congress and other bodies might then begin to take concrete steps to channel police discretion more appropriately.

The Act passed the House of Representatives in March of 1998 by a unanimous vote and was then referred to the Senate Judiciary Committee, but the Committee never voted on the measure or held any hearings.

In April 1999, Congressman Conyers reintroduced the Traffic Stops Statistics Study Act (HR 1443), sponsored in the Senate (S.821) by Frank Lautenberg (D-NJ) and Russell Feingold (D-WI). Passage of the Act should be viewed as a first step toward addressing a difficult problem. While it does not regulate traffic stops, set standards for them, or require implementation of particular policies, it does require the gathering of solid, comprehensive information, so that discussion of the problem might move beyond the question of whether or not the problem exists, to the question of how to fix the problem. [As of October 2001, the bill has not been passed.]

THIRD: Pass Legislation on Traffic Stops in Every State.

Even if the Traffic Stop Statistics Study Act does not become federal law, it has already inspired action at the state and local level. The ACLU calls upon legislators in every state to pass laws that will allow the practice of traffic enforcement to be statistically monitored on an ongoing basis.

In North Carolina, a bill requiring data collection on all traffic stops was passed by overwhelming majorities in both houses of the state legislature and signed into law by the governor on April 21, 1999. This became the first law anywhere in the nation to require the kind of effort that will yield a full, detailed statistical portrait of the use of traffic stops.

Similar bills have been introduced in Pennsylvania, Illinois, Virginia, Massachusetts, New Jersey, Maryland, Arkansas, Texas, Connecticut, Rhode Island, Florida, and California. Efforts are under way in a number of other states to have bills introduced this year.

The Role of the Justice Department

FOURTH: The Justice Department Must Take Steps to Ensure that Racial Profiling Is Not Used in Federally Funded Drug Interdiction Programs.

The U.S. Department of Justice has a moral and legal responsibility to ensure that Operation Pipeline, and every other federally funded crime fighting program, is not encouraging or perpetuating racially biased law enforcement. Drug interdiction goals—important as they may be—do not outweigh the government's obligation to root out racially discriminatory law enforcement practices. Attorney General [Janet] Reno has stated it is "very important to pursue legislation" on data collection. But to date, the Justice Department has not taken a position on the pending federal bills. The Justice Department should actively support the passage of the federal Traffic Stops Statistics Study Act and take the following additional steps:

Restrict future federal funding for Operation Pipeline and other highway drug interdiction programs to local, state and federal agencies that agree to collect and report comprehensive race data on who they stop and who they search.

Conduct a systematic and independent review of Operation Pipeline and all other drug interdiction training programs supported directly or indirectly with any federal funding, to root out any implicit or explicit racial references that encourage improper profiling.

Restrict future federal funding for Operation Pipeline and other highway drug interdiction programs to agencies that agree to implement a series of preventive measures, such as an early warning system that tracks officer behavior and identifies officers who engage in discriminatory practices, a ban on extending the length of a non-consensual traffic stop in order to have drug-sniffing dogs brought to the scene, and the use of written "consent to search" forms that inform drivers of their right to refuse consent to a search.

Collecting Information on Traffic Stops

FIFTH: The 50 Largest U.S. Cities Should Voluntarily Collect Traffic Stop Data.

Jerry Sanders, San Diego's Chief of Police, announced in February [1999] that his department would begin to collect race data on traffic stops without any federal or state requirement or any threat of litigation. In March, Chief William Lansdowne of the San Jose Police Department announced that his department would follow suit, and in April, Portland Police Chief Charles Moose spearheaded an anti-profiling resolution signed by 23 Oregon police agencies—including the State Police—that included a commitment to gather traffic stop data.

These efforts should be replicated in all 50 of the largest cities in the U.S.

The ACLU's Efforts

In April the ACLU of Northern California established a statewide toll-free hotline for victims of discriminatory traffic stops. The hotline number has been publicized on billboards and through a 60-second radio spot. In the first forty-eight hours, the hotline received 200 calls. As of this writing, the count stands at over 1,400.

In mid-May, the national ACLU set up a nationwide DWB hotline—1-877-6-PROFILE. Although the number is just beginning to be publicized through an ad in *Emerge* magazine and the airing of a radio public service announcement, the calls have started to pour in.

Although some police officials are still in denial, we have presented strong and compelling evidence, of both an anecdotal and statistical nature, that racial profiling on our nation's roads and highways is indeed a nationwide problem. As such, it demands a nationwide solution.

The ACLU will continue to monitor incidents of racial profiling closely and will, where appropriate, bring new cases to court. But elected and police officials would be wise to act sooner rather than later.

"Practically all law-enforcement professionals believe in the need for racial profiling."

Racial Profiling Can Be Justified

John Derbyshire

Despite widespread public distaste for the practice, racial profiling is a useful tool in criminal justice, John Derbyshire claims in the following viewpoint. He maintains that although police officers do make assumptions about potential criminals based on prejudice, the practice enables officers to make the best use of their time and resources. According to Derbyshire, arguments against racial profiling ignore the fact that African Americans and Hispanics are more likely to commit crimes and that placing a ban on racial profiling would lead to massive declines in arrests. Derbyshire is a novelist and contributing editor to *National Review*.

As you read, consider the following questions:

1. In Derbyshire's opinion, what event led to an increase in the use of the term "racial profiling"?
2. What did Jesse Jackson confess in 1993?
3. What does Derbyshire think has been the result of America's "hysteria about race"?

"Racial profiling" has become one of the shibboleths of our time. Anyone who wants a public career in the United States must place himself on record as being against it. Thus, ex-senator John Ashcroft, on the eve of his confirmation hearings [for Attorney General]: "It's wrong, inappropriate, shouldn't be done." During the vice-presidential debate [in October 2000,] moderator Bernard Shaw invited the candidates to imagine themselves black victims of racial profiling. Both made the required ritual protestations of outrage. [Joe] Lieberman: "I have a few African-American friends who have gone through this horror, and you know, it makes me want to kind of hit the wall, because it is such an assault on their humanity and their citizenship." [Dick] Cheney: "It's the sense of anger and frustration and rage that would go with knowing that the only reason you were stopped . . . was because of the color of your skin . . ." In the strange, rather depressing, pattern these things always follow nowadays, the American public has speedily swung into line behind the Pied Pipers: Gallup reports that 81 percent of the public disapproves of racial profiling.

The Explosion of a Term

All of which represents an extraordinary level of awareness of, and hostility to, and even passion against ("hit the wall . . .") a practice that, up to about [the mid-1990s,] practically nobody had heard of. It is, in fact, instructive to begin by looking at the history of this shibboleth. . . .

The career of the term "racial profiling" seems to have begun in 1994, but did not really take off until April 1998, when two white New Jersey state troopers pulled over a van for speeding. As they approached the van from behind, it suddenly reversed towards them. The troopers fired eleven shots from their handguns, wounding three of the van's four occupants, who were all black or Hispanic. The troopers, James Kenna and John Hogan, subsequently became poster boys for the "racial profiling" lobbies, facing the same indignities, though so far with less serious consequences, as were endured by the Los Angeles policemen in the Rodney King case: endless investigations, double jeopardy, and so on.

And a shibboleth was born. News-media databases list

only a scattering of instances of the term "racial profiling" from 1994 to 1998. In that latter year, the number hit double digits, and thereafter rose quickly into the hundreds and thousands. Now we all know about it, and we are, of course, all against it.

Arguments for Profiling

Well, not quite all. American courts—including (see below) the U.S. Supreme Court—are not against it. Jurisprudence on the matter is pretty clear: So long as race is only one factor in a generalized approach to the questioning of suspects, it may be considered. And of course, pace Candidate Cheney, it always is only one factor. I have been unable to locate any statistics on the point, but I feel sure that elderly black women are stopped by the police much less often than are young white men.

No Bias in the Justice System

Many studies over the years have determined that when black and white criminals are carefully compared for offense and criminal record, the justice system treats them pretty much the same. As for high rates of incarceration for blacks, compelling evidence from the U.S. government's National Crime Victimization Survey suggests that blacks juvenile and adult are overrepresented in jails because they commit more crimes, not because of judicial bias.

Jared Taylor, *Washington Times*, May 29, 2000.

Even in the political sphere, where truth-telling and independent thinking on matters of race have long been liabilities, there are those who refuse to mouth the required pieties. Alan Keyes, when asked by Larry King if he would be angry with a police officer who pulled him over for being black, replied: "I was raised that everything I did represented my family, my race, and my country. I would be angry with the people giving me a bad reputation."

Practically all law-enforcement professionals believe in the need for racial profiling. In an article on the topic for the *New York Times Magazine* in June 1999, Jeffrey Goldberg interviewed Bernard Parks, chief of the Los Angeles Police

Department. Parks, who is black, asked rhetorically of racial profiling: "Should we play the percentages? . . . It's common sense." Note that date, though. This was pretty much the latest time at which it was possible for a public official to speak truthfully about racial profiling. Law-enforcement professionals were learning the importance of keeping their thoughts to themselves. Four months before the Goldberg piece saw print, New Jersey state-police superintendent Carl Williams, in an interview, said that certain crimes were associated with certain ethnic groups, and that it was naive to think that race was not an issue in policing—both statements, of course, perfectly true. Supt. Williams was fired the same day by Gov. Christie Todd Whitman.

A Negative but Accurate Stereotype

Like other race issues in the U.S., racial profiling is a "tadpole," with an enormous black head and a long but comparatively inconsequential brown, yellow, and red tail. While Hispanic, "Asian-American," and other lesser groups have taken up the "racial profiling" chant with gusto, the crux of the matter is the resentment that black Americans feel toward the attentions of white policemen. By far the largest number of Americans angry about racial profiling are law-abiding black people who feel that they are stopped and questioned because the police regard all black people with undue suspicion. They feel that they are the victims of a negative stereotype.

They are. Unfortunately, a negative stereotype can be correct, and even useful. I was surprised to find, when researching this [viewpoint,] that within the academic field of social psychology there is a large literature on stereotypes, and that much of it—an entire school of thought—holds that stereotypes are essential life tools. On the scientific evidence, the primary function of stereotypes is what researchers call "the reality function." That is, stereotypes are useful tools for dealing with the world. Confronted with a snake or a fawn, our immediate behavior is determined by generalized beliefs—stereotypes—about snakes and fawns. Stereotypes are, in fact, merely one aspect of the mind's ability to make generalizations, without which science and mathematics, not to mention, as the snake/fawn example shows, much of everyday life, would be impossible.

At some level, everybody knows this stuff, even the guardians of the "racial profiling" flame. Jesse Jackson famously, in 1993, confessed that: "There is nothing more painful to me at this stage in my life than to walk down the street and hear footsteps and start thinking about robbery, then look around and see somebody white and feel relieved." Here is Sandra Seegars of the Washington, D.C., Taxicab Commission:

"Late at night, if I saw young black men dressed in a slovenly way, I wouldn't pick them up. . . . And during the day, I'd think twice about it."

Pressed to define "slovenly," Ms. Seegars elaborated thus: "A young black guy with his hat on backwards, shirttail hanging down longer than his coat, baggy pants down below his underwear, and unlaced tennis shoes." Now there's a stereotype for you! Ms. Seegars is, of course, black.

A Commonsense Approach

Law-enforcement officials are simply employing the same stereotypes as you, me, Jesse, and Sandra, but taking the opposite course of action. What we seek to avoid, they pursue. They do this for reasons of simple efficiency. A policeman who concentrates a disproportionate amount of his limited time and resources on young black men is going to uncover far more crimes—and therefore be far more successful in his career—than one who biases his attention toward, say, middle-aged Asian women. It is, as Chief Parks said, common sense.

Similarly with the tail of the tadpole-racial-profiling issues that do not involve black people. China is known to have obtained a top-secret warhead design. Among those with clearance to work on that design are people from various kinds of national and racial background. Which ones should investigators concentrate on? The Swedes? The answer surely is: They should first check out anyone who has family or friends in China, who has made trips to China, or who has met with Chinese officials. This would include me, for example—my father-in-law is an official of the Chinese Communist Party. Would I then have been "racially profiled"?

Statistics Shed Little Light

It is not very surprising to learn that the main fruit of the "racial profiling" hysteria has been a decline in the efficiency of police work. In Philadelphia, a federal court order now requires police to fill out both sides of an 8½-by-11 sheet on every citizen contact. Law-enforcement agencies nationwide are engaged in similar statistics-gathering exercises, under pressure from federal lawmakers like U.S. Rep. John Conyers, who has announced that he will introduce a bill to force police agencies to keep detailed information about traffic stops. ("The struggle goes on," declared Rep. Conyers. The struggle that is going on, it sometimes seems, is a struggle to prevent our police forces from accomplishing any useful work at all.)

The mountain of statistics that is being brought forth by all this panic does not, on the evidence so far, seem likely to shed much light on what is happening. The numbers have a way of leading off into infinite regresses of uncertainty. The city of San Jose, Calif., for example, discovered that, yes, the percentage of blacks being stopped was higher than their representation in the city's population. Ah, but patrol cars were computer-assigned to high-crime districts, which are mainly inhabited by minorities. So that over-representation might actually be an under-representation! But then, minorities have fewer cars. . . .

Notwithstanding the extreme difficulty of finding out what is actually happening, we can at least seek some moral and philosophical grounds on which to take a stand either for or against racial profiling. I am going to take it as a given that most readers of this article will be of a conservative inclination, and shall offer only those arguments likely to appeal to persons so inclined. If you seek arguments of other kinds, they are not hard to find—just pick up your newspaper or turn on your TV.

Persuasive Arguments Against Profiling

Of arguments against racial profiling, probably the ones most persuasive to a conservative are the ones from libertarianism. Many of the stop-and-search cases that brought this matter into the headlines were part of the so-called war on drugs.

116

The police procedures behind them were ratified by court decisions of the 1980s, themselves mostly responding to the rising tide of illegal narcotics. In *U.S. vs. Montoya De Hernandez* (1985) for example, Chief Justice [William] Rehnquist validated the detention of a suspected "balloon swallowing" drug courier until the material had passed through her system, by noting previous invasions upheld by the Court:

[F]irst class mail may be opened without a warrant on less than probable cause. . . . Automotive travellers may be stopped . . . near the border without individualized suspicion even if the stop is based largely on ethnicity. . . .

(My italics.) The Chief Justice further noted that these incursions are in response to "the veritable national crisis in law enforcement caused by smuggling of illegal narcotics." Many on the political Right feel that the war on drugs is at best misguided, at worst a moral and constitutional disaster. Yet it is naive to imagine that the "racial profiling" hubbub would go away, or even much diminish, if all state and federal drug laws were repealed tomorrow. Black and Hispanic Americans would still be committing crimes at rates higher than citizens of other races. The differential criminality of various ethnic groups is not only, or even mainly, located in drug crimes. In 1997, for example, blacks, who are 13 percent of the U.S. population, comprised 35 percent of those arrested for embezzlement. (It is not generally appreciated that black Americans commit higher levels not only of "street crime," but also of white-collar crime.)

Even without the drug war, diligent police officers would still, therefore, be correct to regard black and Hispanic citizens—other factors duly considered—as more likely to be breaking the law. The Chinese government would still be trying to recruit spies exclusively from among Chinese-born Americans. (The Chinese Communist Party is, in this respect, the keenest "racial profiler" of all.) The Amadou Diallo case—the police were looking for a rapist—would still have happened.

A Response to Randall Kennedy

The best non-libertarian argument against racial profiling is the one from equality before the law. This has been most cogently presented by Prof. Randall Kennedy of Harvard. Kennedy concedes most of the points I have made. Yes, he says:

> Statistics abundantly confirm that African Americans— and particularly young black men—commit a dramatically disproportionate share of street crime in the United States. This is a sociological fact, not a figment of the media's (or the police's) racist imagination. In recent years, for example, victims of crime report blacks as the perpetrators in around 25 percent of the violent crimes suffered, although blacks constitute only about twelve percent of the nation's population.

And yes, says Prof. Kennedy, outlawing racial profiling will reduce the efficiency of police work. Nonetheless, for constitutional and moral reasons we should outlaw the practice. If this places extra burdens on law enforcement, well, "racial equality, like all good things in life, costs something; it does not come for free."

There are two problems with this. The first is that Kennedy has minimized the black-white difference in criminality, and therefore that "cost." I don't know where his 25 percent comes from, or what "recent years" means, but I do know that in Department of Justice figures for 1997, victims report 60 percent of robberies as having been committed by black persons. In that same year, a black American was eight times more likely than a non-black to commit homicide— and "non-black" here includes Hispanics, not broken out separately in these figures. A racial-profiling ban, under which police officers were required to stop and question suspects in precise proportion to their demographic representation (in what? the precinct population? the state population? the national population?), would lead to massive inefficiencies in police work. Which is to say, massive declines in the apprehension of criminals.

The other problem is with the special status that Prof. Kennedy accords to race. Kennedy: "Racial distinctions are and should be different from other lines of social stratification." Thus, if it can be shown, as it surely can, that state troopers stop young people more than old people, relative to young people's numerical representation on the road being patrolled, that is of no consequence. If they stop black people more than white people, on the same criterion, that is of large consequence. This, in spite of the fact that the categories "age" and "race" are both rather fuzzy (define "young") and are both useful predictors of criminality. In spite of the fact, too, that the principle of equality before the law does not, and up to now has never been thought to, guarantee equal outcomes for any law-enforcement process, only that a citizen who has come under reasonable suspicion will be treated fairly.

It is on this special status accorded to race that, I believe, we have gone most seriously astray. I am willing, in fact, to say much more than this: In the matter of race, I think the Anglo-Saxon world has taken leave of its senses. The campaign to ban racial profiling is, as I see it, a part of that large, broad-fronted assault on common sense that our over-educated, over-lawyered society has been enduring for some forty years now, and whose roots are in a fanatical egalitarianism, a grim determination not to face up to the realities of group differences, a theological attachment to the doctrine that the sole and sufficient explanation for all such differences is "racism"—which is to say, the malice and cruelty of white people—and a nursed and petted guilt towards the behavior of our ancestors.

Confronting Race Hysteria

At present, Americans are drifting away from the concept of belonging to a single nation. I do not think this drift will be arrested until we can shed the idea that deference to the sensitivities of racial minorities—however overwrought those sensitivities may be, however over-stimulated by unscrupulous mountebanks, however disconnected from reality—trumps every other consideration, including even the maintenance of social order. To shed that idea, we must confront our national hysteria about race, which causes large numbers of otherwise sane people to believe that the hearts of their fellow citizens are filled with malice towards them. So long as we continue to pander to that poisonous, preposterous belief, we shall only wander off deeper into a wilderness of division, mistrust, and institutionalized rancor—that wilderness, the most freshly painted signpost to which bears the legend RACIAL PROFILING.

*"Mandatory minimum sentencing laws . . .
unfairly punish African American and
Hispanic defendants."*

Mandatory Minimum
Sentencing Laws Are Unfair

Maxine Waters

Laws that impose mandatory minimum sentences for drug
sales and possession are unfair to minorities, Maxine Waters
argues in the following viewpoint. According to Waters,
these laws are particularly biased because they impose longer
sentences on possession of crack cocaine, which is cheaper
and more common in poor communities, than on possession
of powder cocaine, whose users are more likely to be white.
Waters also asserts that African Americans are disproportionately arrested and sentenced for drug use and possession.
She states that instead of mandatory minimum sentences,
the drug problem should be addressed by developing programs that will help young people. Waters is a Democratic
congresswoman from California.

As you read, consider the following questions:

1. According to Waters, how many grams of powder
   cocaine would a person have to possess to receive the
   same sentence as someone with five grams of crack
   cocaine?
2. What percentage of people in prison for drug-related
   offenses are African American, according to statistics
   cited by the author?
3. How does Waters believe youth who come in contact
   with the justice system should be treated?

When Congress passed its latest slew of mandatory minimum sentencing laws in the 1980s, the notion was to get tough on crime, especially drug-related crimes. The plan was to unclog the court system, jail drug kingpins who were preying on our nation's young people, and prevent "liberal" judges from letting criminals off too easily.

The "war on drugs," "get tough on crime," "three strikes, you're out" slogans that politicians used so well on the campaign trail have been sadly crafted into laws with little consideration for their human consequences.

The Ill Effects of Mandatory Minimum Laws

For more than two decades as an elected official, I have witnessed the negative impact of wrong-minded public policy on black communities and, especially, on black youth. Too often, legislators vote on bills without fully understanding their impact on individuals. In many cases, they would prefer not to put a face on those who are affected.

I believe that unless we fully understand how legislation impacts the lives of the people we govern, we are doomed to pass laws that create more problems than they solve. This is most evident when we examine how mandatory minimum sentencing laws impact poor communities.

These mandatory minimum laws remove from the hands of judges and other court officials the ability to examine the individual circumstances of each case before sentencing. A judge's discretion can mean the difference between a young person going to jail and having his or her life irreparably damaged or being placed in a program that might have a chance to save a human being.

While judges cannot be caseworkers, they can look at the circumstances of a young offender's life to make rational and reasoned evaluations of someone's risk to society. For example, a teenage female addict, called a "strawberry" on the streets of South Central Los Angeles because she sells her body to support her habit, needs help and intervention, not a five-year mandatory minimum prison term. A young crack-addicted mother who passes her habit to her infant needs help—first to kick her own habit and then with educational and employment opportunities—so that she can support her child.

Mandatory minimum sentencing laws do little to help in cases like these; they only punish. And, more often than not, they unfairly punish African American and Hispanic defendants as compared to whites who commit similar crimes. Nowhere is this more evident than when we examine the disparate sentencing laws surrounding the possession or distribution of crack cocaine versus powder cocaine.

Crack Versus Cocaine

In 1986 and 1988, Congress mandated harsher sentencing for crack cocaine distributors and users than for powder cocaine, despite the fact that they are simply different forms of the same illegal drug. Crack cocaine, a cheaper version of cocaine than powder, is more commonly found in poor communities.

Under the current sentencing mandates passed by Congress, a young person convicted of trafficking in five grams of crack cocaine receives a five-year mandatory minimum penalty. A young person selling the same amount of powder cocaine would be charged with a misdemeanor offense punishable by a maximum of one year. It would take possession of 500 grams of powder cocaine to receive the same five-year mandatory sentence the defendant with 5 grams of crack receives. This statutory 100 to 1 ratio of powder to crack has relegated a disproportionate number of black and Hispanic youth to long-term prison sentences that stigmatize them for life.

The recommendation by Attorney General Janet Reno to reduce the disparity to a 10 to 1 ratio is an improvement, but does not end the imbalance. Indeed, the rationale presented by Reno to reduce the disparity to 10 to 1 is equally persuasive when applied to the question of eliminating any sentencing disparities between crack and powder cocaine. The violence associated with crack dealing has dropped over the past few years. There is an almost even split between crack users and powder users, and the treatment programs for crack and powder users are similar, with similar success rates.

In addition, both Attorney General Reno and drug czar General [Barry] McCaffrey concede that the disparity has led to selective prosecution of African-American and Hispanic young men within the federal courts. This is true even though "crack cocaine use is more prevalent among young whites than among young blacks," according to the Office of National Drug Control Policy. In 1994, for example, "a larger percentage (3.2%) of whites aged 18–25 used crack cocaine than did blacks in the same age group (1.8%). Additionally, in 1994, a larger percentage of whites in age groups 12–17, 18–25 and 26–34 used cocaine than did blacks in the same age (group)." Yet, "blacks and non-whites are sentenced for crack violations disproportionately."

Comparison of Drug Use and Arrests by Race

| Year | Black | | White | |
	Percent of Current Drug Users	Percent of Drug Arrests	Percent of Current Drug Users	Percent of Drug Arrests
1979	10.8%	21.8%	87.8%	76.7%
1985	12.4%	30%	86.6%	68.9%
1991	15.3%	41%	83.9%	58.1%
1992	11.9%	39.6%	87.1%	59.4%
1993	12.1%	39.3%	87%	59.8%
1994	15%	0	84%	60.6%
1995	16.2%	36.9%	82.7%	62.1%
1996	15.4%	38.4%	83.5%	60.4%
1997	14.9%	36.8%	83.9%	62%
1998	16.9%	37.3%	82%	61.5%

Compiled from Federal Bureau of Investigation, *Uniform Crime Reports*, various years, and Substance Abuse and Mental Health Services Administration, *Summary of Findings from the 1998 National Household Survey on Drug Abuse* (U.S. Department of Health and Human Services, 1999).

The impact of the sentencing disparities is staggering. Today, African-American males make up 6 percent of the American population and only 15 percent of the drug-using population. Yet, they now represent 35 percent of drug arrests, 55 percent of drug convictions and 74 percent of those serving prison sentences for drug-related offenses. One in three black males between the ages of 20 and 29 is under criminal justice control. One in 15 is incarcerated. Ninety-four percent of the crack offenders in federal courts are African American. In practice, the "war on drugs" has become synonymous with a war on black communities.

In addition, this so-called war has disenfranchised large

segments of African Americans by taking away their right to vote. A study by the Sentencing Project estimated that 1.46 million black males have lost the right to vote due to a felony conviction.

Correcting the Disparity

[In 1995,] we attempted to remove the disparities between the sentencing for crack cocaine offenses and powder cocaine offenses. The United States Sentencing Commission reported that there was no scientific basis for the disparity and acknowledged that blacks were more heavily impacted by the disparity than whites. Despite these arguments, Congress rejected the recommendations by a vote of 332-83. Ironically, the Sentencing Commission was created specifically to ensure that sentencing policy in our nation is fairly and equitably administered and protected from the political world.

In addition to fighting to correct the harsh and unfair sentencing disparities between crack and powder cocaine, the Congressional Black Caucus (CBC) has proposed several initiatives to address the drug problem in our communities.

Instead of dismantling economic and educational opportunities for poor communities, we should target more resources toward programs that work to rebuild our neighborhoods.

How to Treat Drug Offenders

Currently, the federal government spends $15 billion each year on law enforcement, treatment and prevention programs in its "war on drugs." The CBC anti-drug initiative calls for a $200 million allocation for drug courts to treat low-level or first-time non-violent drug offenders, especially youth. There are successful drug court programs, such as those in New York City, that demonstrate the important role these programs can play in helping young people solve drug-related problems.

We must give special attention to youth who come into contact with both the juvenile justice and the criminal justice system. Helping young people through mentoring and educational programs at an early age is a critical component in crime prevention programs.

We must treat prisoners for their drug addictions. Given

the overwhelming rise in the number of drug offenders serving mandatory minimum sentences and the number of these prisoners who will be released from prison, treating prisoners for their drug addiction is in society's best interest.

As we look for answers, we must remember that all problems have real human faces. Our solutions must also.

"Mandatory minimum sentences for drug dealers are logical and desirable."

Mandatory Minimum Sentencing Laws Are Desirable

George Allen

In the following testimony, George Allen asserts that mandatory minimum sentences for drug dealers are desirable and should be increased. He contends that these sentences are justified because illegal drug traffic leads to more crime and an increased rate of adolescent drug use. Allen also argues that increasing the punishment for powder cocaine, as well as other drugs, is the best way to eliminate the disparity that exists between sentences for possession of crack cocaine and sentences for possession of powder cocaine. Allen is a former governor of Virginia. The following viewpoint was taken from testimony he gave before the House Subcommittee on Criminal Justice, Drug Policy, and Human Resources in May 2000.

As you read, consider the following questions:

1. According to reports cited by Allen, what proportion of youth between the ages of twelve and seventeen are using drugs?
2. What message does Allen believe America should send to drug dealers?
3. What does the author think should be done to mandatory minimum sentences at the federal level?

From George Allen's testimony before the House Subcommittee on Criminal Justice, Drug Policy, and Human Resources, May 11, 2000.

Thank you, Mr. Chairman [Dan Burton], and members of the committee. I very much appreciate the opportunity and thank you for the invitation to testify today. I commend the subcommittee's interest in looking at how the Federal Government can partner with the States and localities in combating the scourge of illegal drugs, in trying to stop them and also stop them from ruining more lives.

Logical and Desirable Sentences

Mr. Chairman, I fully endorse the sentiments that were expressed in your opening statement. I do believe the mandatory minimum sentences for drug dealers are logical and desirable and that mandatory sentences, in my view, ought to be increased, especially for those who sell drugs to children, so that they serve even longer sentences in those situations.

Now mandatory minimum sentences, as a general rule, reflect the desires of people in a State or in America in the sense that it comes from Washington, and it is their sense of outrage over certain crimes. There are mandatory minimum sentences not just in dealing with drug dealing but also there are mandatory minimum sentences for assaulting a police officer, as opposed to assaulting a citizen who is not a law officer. There are mandatory minimum sentences for second drunk driving offenses. There are mandatory minimum sentences for habitual offenders and also mandatory minimums, I think very appropriate, for the use of a firearm in commission of a crime.

Now, drugs breed so much of the crime. In fact, the majority of all crime is drug-related. The chairman mentioned, as did Congressman [Elijah] Cummings, [a] situation here in the District where [an] individual is indicted who had been involved in 15 murders, besides having a reign of terror as far as drug dealing.

Now, you also need to think of how many other people were victimized by his minions or part of his network and people who have been robbed, individually robbed, or their homes broken into, their businesses broken into or their cars broken into from people who are addicted to drugs and have to find ways to pay for that addiction.

Now, drug use is on the rise. It was declining maybe in the

1980s but we are seeing it rising. It is rising among college students. It is rising among high school students, even in middle schools. Reports from the Federal Government and national reports show that between the ages of 12 and 17, 1 out of every 10 youngsters between that age group are currently using drugs.

Black Congresspersons and the Anti–Drug Abuse Act

One might have thought that for those who are suspicious of the aims and sentiments that guided the design of the Anti–Drug Abuse Act, the positions and statements of *black* members of Congress would be of some importance. But Judge [Clyde S.] Cahill and virtually all of the rest of the critics who have condemned as racist the crack-powder distinction have failed to take into account the opinions of the members of Congress who concerned themselves most intently and consistently with elevating the fortunes of African-Americans, namely the black members of Congress. They have rendered the blacks in Congress invisible. This is not to say that the opinions of black members of Congress should be viewed as dispositive. Persons of any hue can be wrong, opportunistic, or racially prejudiced even with respect to people of their own racial background. Still, it would be useful to some extent to know where the black members of Congress have stood on the matter. The claim that illicit racial beliefs and perceptions animated the enactment of the crack-powder distinction would surely be strengthened if all or even most of the black members of Congress had objected to the statute on racial grounds.

The fact is, however, that eleven of the twenty-one blacks who were then members of the House of Representatives voted in favor of the law which created the 100-to-1 crack-powder differential.

Randall Kennedy, *Race, Crime, and the Law*, 1997.

The age of heroin use, first-time heroin use—early in 1990, the average age for first-time use was around 26, 27 years old. It is now at 17 years old for heroin use.

Now Mr. Chairman and members of the committee, I am the father of an 11-year-old daughter and younger kids than that, but this is very worrisome to me as a parent and I think to parents all across America. It is not just an issue, though, in urban areas; it is an issue in rural areas; it is an issue in suburban areas, as well, and we must do everything we can to keep the scourge of drugs from dimming and diminishing the great promise and bright future that all our children should have.

Virginia's Experience

Now, I would like to share with you some of our experiences in Virginia and some of the things that clearly do work. What we did is we abolished the lenient, dishonest parole system. Criminals, felons, especially violent criminals, are serving much longer sentences, and it is common sense. The results are that the crime rates are way down in Virginia. Virginia's crime rates are lower than the national average.

And the effort in Virginia I think can be translated into what you all are facing here as you make these decisions, especially when you realize how much drugs are involved in crime activity. Drugs obviously breed crime. Drugs destroy young lives, especially young lives, and also tear families apart.

I think that we need to send a message that we are serious, that as far as fighting these drug dealers, that we want you out of our neighborhoods, out of our communities, out of circulation, and especially we want you out of reach of our children.

So I proposed an idea called project drug exile. It builds upon what we have done in Virginia, and you had our attorney general, Mark Early, speak to this committee just a few months ago on project exile, which was cracking down on those possessing illegal drugs—excuse me—illegal guns, and that has worked very well in the city of Richmond.

Now, project drug exile builds upon that approach in that you have more law enforcement, you have more prosecution and when people are caught, then they get mandatory sentencing.

Sentences Should Be Increased

Congressman Cummings and Congresswoman [Janice] Schakowsky brought up the disparities as far as the powder cocaine versus crack cocaine. Yes, there is that discriminatory result in sentencing. My view is that what ought to be done is do not diminish the punishment for using crack cocaine; you ought to increase the punishment for those who are selling powder cocaine and, in fact, Ecstasy or methamphetamines like Crystal Meth or Ice.

I also recommend that the committee increase the mandatory minimum sentences at the Federal level—in fact, double them, double the mandatory minimums for those who are selling drugs to minors. Also, I think you ought to raise the penalty for the lethal combination of the illegal possession of a firearm and illegal drugs, increase that penalty to 7 years.

So Mr. Chairman and members of the committee, I have no compassion or any sympathy whatsoever for these drug dealers who peddle this poison to our children. We ought to treat them as if they are forcing them to use rat poison because the results can be very much the same.

So I think what needs to be done is we need to have multifaceted, consistent enforcement. We need strong incapacitation because if somebody is behind bars, they cannot be running their operations; they cannot be harming the lives of our loved ones, our families, and ruining our communities.

So I thank you again for your interest and hope that this committee can go forth to help make our communities, working with the States, working with localities, safer places for our children to live and play and learn and us to raise our families. Thank you, Mr. Chairman.

"[The Miranda *rule] has done good, and it has not done the harm that some people feared when it was decided."*

Miranda Protects Defendants

John P. Frank

In the following viewpoint, John P. Frank argues that the U.S. Supreme Court made the correct decision on June 26, 2000, when it ruled that the *Miranda* warning should not be overturned. According to Frank, *Miranda* protects a defendant's right against self-incrimination by preventing police from using torture to obtain false confessions. He asserts that despite the efforts of Congress to weaken *Miranda*, the law has been proven sound and helpful. Frank argued for Ernesto Miranda in the 1966 Supreme Court case *Miranda v. Arizona.*

As you read, consider the following questions:

1. According to Frank, what makes the safeguard of the Fifth Amendment meaningless?
2. How were African American defendants treated in Bessemer, Alabama, as detailed by Justice Hugo Black?
3. In Frank's opinion, what is every American entitled to know?

M iranda lives. Well, not the person. He [Ernesto Miranda] died in a tavern brawl many years ago. The *Miranda* rule—the requirement that defendants must be told that "you have the right to remain silent and to request counsel"— was reaffirmed by the U.S. Supreme Court on June 26, 2000.

Precisely what are we talking about? The fifth amendment to the U.S. Constitution provides that no person can testify against himself. This safeguard is meaningless if, before he gets to court, a witness has made damaging statements. By the time he gets to court, the constitutional protection will do him no good.

The Origin and Purpose of *Miranda*

The *Miranda* case, which went to the Supreme Court from Arizona, established the rule that any person in custody must be told of his constitutional rights, and that if he was not, no statement he makes can be used against him ever.

This requirement came directly from the practice of the FBI. That agency, the prime police force in the country, had a fixed practice of telling people of their constitutional rights. What the Supreme Court did in *Miranda* was to require the countless state, city and county police officials throughout the country to do the same thing.

The purpose of the *Miranda* rule is to prevent forced confessions or, to put it more bluntly, torture. It may be easier to get people to talk by beating them with a strap or rubbing pepper in their eyes. This has been done not only in communist or fascist countries, but in America as well. When Justice Hugo Black, one of the justices in the *Miranda* case, was a young prosecuting attorney in Alabama, he noticed that he was getting an astonishing large number of confessions from African-American defendants in Bessemer, Alabama. This is because the defendants there, when they were brought to the police station, were strapped to a door and beaten until they confessed; and one of the problems is that people under torture may confess to stop the torture, whether they did it or not.

Chief Justice Earl Warren wrote the *Miranda* decision, and as attorney general and governor of California, he had seen the same kinds of abuse.

Attempts to Restrict *Miranda*

Immediately after *Miranda* was decided, there was considerable concern that guilty people might escape justice. Congress passed a statute restricting the Miranda rights. That statute had been ignored until 1999, when a federal court dug it up and applied it. It is that statute which was before the Supreme Court in the decision [in 2000].

In the intervening 34 years, the *Miranda* rule has proved to be sound police tactics. It has done good, and it has not done the harm that some people feared when it was decided.

A question of whether that act of Congress, restricting Miranda rights, was itself constitutional, finally reached the Supreme Court [in 2000]. On June 26, the Supreme Court ruled, 7-to-2, in an opinion by Chief Justice William Rehnquist, reaffirmed the *Miranda* rules and held unconstitutional an act of Congress that attempted to water them down.

Sargent. © 1999 by The Austin American Statesman. Reprinted by permission of Universal Press Syndicate. All rights reserved.

"Coerced confessions are inherently untrustworthy," Rehnquist wrote in recognizing the problem: In reviewing earlier decisions, he said that they had held that "even without employing brutality or the third-degree," questioning a

133

person who is in custody "exacts a heavy toll on individual liberty and trades on the weakness of individuals." *Miranda*, he said, requires that you at least give a suspect "four warnings" known as the "Miranda rights."

Miranda Is Part of American Culture

The main point of the chief justice was that in the 34-year period since *Miranda*, law enforcement systems of the country have adjusted to it. Its warnings, he said, have "become part of our national culture."

As a result, he said, it is now clearly established that "unwarned statements may not be used as evidence in the prosecution's case."

This 7-to-2 opinion is so decisive that it should establish for the future that every person in America, rich or poor, educated or uneducated, is governed by the Constitution. Every person in the United States, rich or poor, educated or uneducated, is entitled to know what is in the Constitution. *Miranda* says no more than this, but, as much as the Supreme Court of the United States can make it so, this will ever be our law.

"Exactly how many murderers and armed robbers would the Court find it worth setting free in the interests of retaining the Miranda *rule?"*

The Supreme Court Should Not Have Upheld *Miranda*

Paul G. Cassell

In 1966, the U.S. Supreme Court ruled in *Miranda v. Arizona* that people under arrest must be informed of their rights before they can be questioned by the police. On June 26, 2000, the U.S. Supreme Court ruled 7-2 in *Dickerson v. United States* that *Miranda* should continue to govern whether statements made by defendants during interrogation can be admissible in court. In the following viewpoint, Paul G. Cassell criticizes the court's decision. He contends that *Miranda* should have been overturned because of the harm it has caused law enforcement by hampering the ability of police officers to solve crimes. According to Cassell, the court ought to have considered alternatives to *Miranda*, such as videotaping police questioning. Cassell is a professor of law at the University of Utah and a leading critic of *Miranda*.

As you read, consider the following questions:

1. What do defenders of *Miranda* claim are its benefits?
2. According to the author, how would videotaping reduce wrongful convictions?
3. What is the "true tragedy of Dickerson," in Cassell's view?

Excerpted from "The Paths Not Taken: The Supreme Court's Failures in Dickerson," by Paul G. Cassell, *Michigan Law Review*, March 2001. Copyright © 2001 by *Michigan Law Review*. Reprinted with permission.

T he Court took the easy way out [in the *Dickerson* deci-
sion]—it dodged the issue.

In short, what the Court could have said in *Dickerson* was
this: There is a factual question about whether *Miranda* has
harmed legitimate law enforcement efforts. Congress is the
branch of government charged with resolving such questions. Congress held hearings on this subject and reasonably concluded that *Miranda* was seriously hampering police efforts to solve crime and convict criminals. As a result,
what would have been the result of *Dickerson* properly ac-
knowledging that there was harm to law enforcement from
Miranda? Does it necessarily follow that *Miranda* should
have been overruled? Such harm would, at a minimum, be
relevant to the Court's calculation whether to retain *Miranda* or return to the earlier voluntariness regime. The
Court's stare decisis jurisprudence explicitly acknowledges
the relevance of real-world effects. In deciding whether to
overrule *Roe v. Wade*, for instance, the controlling opinion
from the Court described the decision to overrule as "cus-
tomarily informed by a series of prudential and respective
costs of reaffirming and overruling a prior case." On this
view, the "costs" of the *Miranda* rules are indisputably part
of the stare decisis calculation.

The Advantages and Disadvantages of *Miranda*

Starting from the proper premise that Congress reasonably
found *Miranda* to entail significant costs, it would have been
interesting to see how the Court then assessed the competing issues. Just exactly how many murderers and armed robbers would the Court find it worth setting free in the interests of retaining the *Miranda* rule? The Court has not
proven particularly adept at assessing such tradeoffs. In *Miranda* itself, for example, the Court appeared to balance
competing concerns in ways that most Americans found ob-
jectionable. Rather than linger over such difficult issues, it is
understandable that the Court simply chose to toss off cur-
sory assertions about *Miranda*'s limited harm before gallop-
ing off to its disposition, leaving the hard questions to be answered in, . . . er . . . , later law review symposia.

But assuming that the Court had recognized *Miranda*'s

harms, would overruling the decision have necessarily followed? Against *Miranda*'s disadvantages, the Court would have needed to assay the advantages. Defenders of *Miranda* have claimed, for example, that *Miranda* entails such benefits as reducing police coercion during the questioning of suspects and communicating to suspects "our societal commitment to restraint in an area in which emotions easily run uncontrolled." Balancing these advantages against *Miranda*'s disadvantages would have been difficult not only because of disagreement about the existence of these benefits, but more generally because of a commensurability problem—these concerns are not susceptible to evaluation on a common scale.

Ignoring Alternatives to *Miranda*

A critique of *Dickerson* for reaching one conclusion or the other on such contentious issues would probably never command broad assent. But it seems to me that an alternative critique is available, which might draw wider approval. Even assuming that the Court properly struck down [sections] 3501 [Congress' alternative to *Miranda*], the *Dickerson* opinion is deficient in failing to discuss possible alternatives to *Miranda* that Congress could adopt. *Dickerson*'s silence on reasonable alternatives starkly contrasts with *City of Chicago v. Morales*, a case from the preceding Term. In *Morales*, the Court struck down Chicago's gang-loitering ordinance essentially on vagueness grounds. But the swing justices—Justice O'Connor joined by Justice Breyer— wrote a concurring opinion explaining how Chicago could cure the defects. This led Chicago to adopt a new ordinance conforming precisely to the requirements spelled out in the concurring opinion. Justice O'Connor's *Morales* concurrence illustrates what Professor Erik Luna has helpfully called a "constitutional roadmap." The controlling justices on the Court gave guidance to Chicago so that Chicago's city council could pass an ordinance that complied with the Constitution.

Dickerson should have followed Justice O'Connor's approach in *Morales*—offering some instruction about why [sections] 3501 and related enactments were defective and what the Congress needed to do to supplement them. Perhaps some constitutional purists will demur. Touting passive virtues and the like, they will suggest that the Court should take the cases one at a time, leaving the possibility of alternatives to be resolved in a proper case and controversy. In many circumstances, such arguments for judicial restraint might have considerable force. But in the particular context of *Miranda*, the case for roadmapping becomes compelling. *Miranda* is "a decision without a past"—an opinion without foundation in the previous court precedents. As a result, in contrast with other bodies of law, conscientious legislators lack authoritative guidance for any effort to determine what alternatives might satisfy the constitutional requirements. Dickerson offers no help to the legislature, since it merely offers an unexplained "thumbs down" to the alternative before it, [sections] 3501. Perhaps uncertainty might be tolerable if the legislature could simply authorize a test case to explore the acceptability of alternatives to *Miranda*. But the ability to test alternatives before the Court is limited. A decision by a police agency to depart from *Miranda* and try some different device risks suppression of a confession. If applied more widely—as might be necessary to obtain appellate review of the issue—it runs the risk of wholesale reversal of criminal convictions, years after the fact.

Dickerson was clearly an "opportunity missed" to make positive reforms, and will continue the "petrification" of the law of pretrial interrogation in this country. For those who think *Miranda* is the be-all and end-all of rules for this area, perhaps this result will be applauded. But it would be odd if a 1966, 5-4 decision by the Supreme Court embodied the best possible resolution of the competing concerns. . . .

Replacing *Miranda* with Videotape

This [viewpoint] also provides considerable evidence for the solution to *Miranda* defects—the proverbial "win-win" solution that properly protects both suspects and society's legitimate interests. *Dickerson* should have suggested to Congress that it consider replacing *Miranda* with a system of videotaping police questioning. Videotaping of interrogations improves on *Miranda* by providing an objective record of what happened inside the stationhouse. Videotaping thus allows courts to police the lines between proper and improper tactics, rather than leaving that job to others. Videotaping would also help reduce the number of wrongful convictions from false confessions by revealing those rare cases where suspects (particularly the mentally retarded) are led to confess to crimes they did not commit. I have argued elsewhere that videotaping could largely replace the Miranda regime.

A Preposterous Decision

History and precedent aside, the decision in *Miranda*, if read as an explication of what the Constitution requires, is preposterous. There is, for example, simply no basis in reason for concluding that a response to the very first question asked, by a suspect who already knows all of the rights described in the Miranda warning, is anything other than a volitional act. And even if one assumes that the elimination of compulsion absolutely requires informing even the most knowledgeable suspect of his right to remain silent, it cannot conceivably require the right to have counsel present. There is a world of difference, which the Court recognized under the traditional voluntariness test but ignored in *Miranda*, between compelling a suspect to incriminate himself and preventing him from foolishly doing so of his own accord. Only the latter (which is not required by the Constitution) could explain the Court's inclusion of a right to counsel and the requirement that it, too, be knowingly and intelligently waived. Counsel's presence is not required to tell the suspect that he need not speak; the interrogators can do that. The only good reason for having counsel there is that he can be counted on to advise the suspect that he should not speak.

Justice Antonin Scalia, dissenting opinion in *Dickerson v. United States*, June 26, 2000.

Other commentators—including prominently Stephen Schulhofer, Welsh White, and Richard Leo—have urged that videotaping should supplement the Miranda regime. And between these varying positions there certainly are a range of possibilities for using videotaping in combination with various parts of the Miranda regime. Yet the Court's opinion in *Dickerson* contains not even the briefest discussion of this (or other) alternatives—it gives no roadmap for legislators to follow. The result, not surprisingly, has been inaction in Congress and legislatures on possible alternatives to *Miranda*.

Reasonable people can disagree about exactly which of these various alternatives would have been preferable. But if this viewpoint suggests nothing else, it is that society has compelling reasons constantly to examine how to improve its regulations of police interrogation. *Miranda* itself recognizes this point. *Miranda* went out of its way pointedly to "encourage Congress and the States to continue their laudable search for increasingly effective ways of protecting the rights of the individual while promoting efficient enforcement of our criminal laws." The *Miranda* Court explained that "we cannot say that the Constitution necessarily requires adherence to any particular solution" to the issues lurking in police questioning of suspects. "Our decision," promised *Miranda*, "in no way creates a constitutional straitjacket which will handicap sound efforts at reform, nor is it intended to have that effect.

Thirty-four years later, the *Dickerson* Court chose not to repeat this encouragement to Congress and the states; nor did it renew *Miranda*'s promise to avoid creating a constitutional straitjacket. Instead, making a virtue out of vice, *Dickerson* tells us that the *Miranda* procedures have become part of our "national culture"—a cultural straitjacket presumably not susceptible to reform. *Miranda* needs reform. . . . The true tragedy of *Dickerson* is, then, not the path that the Court chose—but the paths that it seemingly foreclosed.

> "Pursuing and punishing criminals makes little sense unless society does so in a manner that fully respects the rights of their victims."

The United States Needs a Constitutional Amendment to Protect Crime Victims

Laurence H. Tribe

Laurence H. Tribe argues in the following viewpoint that victims of crime are entitled to a constitutional amendment that ensures they will not be further victimized by the criminal justice system. Tribe contends that victims should be allowed to observe and participate in all relevant criminal trial proceedings because such participation parallels the rights of citizens to take part in government processes that affect their lives. He concludes that a carefully constructed victims' rights amendment would be more effective than the laws that many states have enacted. Tribe is a professor of law at Harvard University.

As you read, consider the following questions:

1. What does Tribe believe are the central concerns of the Constitution?
2. Why does the author believe the *Richmond Newspapers* case is important?
3. According to Tribe, why would rules protecting victims' rights not be as effective as a constitutional amendment?

B eginning with the premise that the Constitution should not be amended lightly and should never be amended to achieve short-term, partisan, or purely policy objectives, I would argue that a constitutional amendment is appropriate only when the goal involves (1) a needed change in government structure, or (2) a needed recognition of a basic human right where (a) the right is one that people widely agree deserves serious and permanent respect, (b) the right is one that is insufficiently protected under existing law, (c) the right is one that cannot be adequately protected through purely political action such as state or federal legislation and/or regulation, (d) the right is one whose inclusion in the U.S. Constitution would not distort or endanger basic principles of the separation of powers among the federal branches, or the division of powers between the national and state governments, and (e) the right would be judicially enforceable without creating open-ended or otherwise unacceptable funding obligations.

Victims' Rights Are Human Rights

I believe that a properly drafted victims' rights amendment would meet these criteria. The rights in question—rights of crime victims not to be victimized yet again through the processes by which government bodies and officials prosecute, punish, and release the accused or convicted offender—are indisputably basic human rights against government, rights that any civilized system of justice would aspire to protect and strive never to violate. To protect these rights of victims does not entail constitutionalizing the rights of private citizens against other private citizens; for it is not the private citizen accused of crime by state or federal authorities who is the source of the violations that victims' rights advocates hope to address with a constitutional amendment in this area. Rather, it is the government authorities themselves—those who pursue (or release) the accused or convicted criminal with insufficient attention to the concerns of the victim— who are sometimes guilty of the kinds of violations that a properly drawn amendment would prohibit.

Pursuing and punishing criminals makes little sense unless society does so in a manner that fully respects the rights of their victims to be accorded dignity and respect, to be treated fairly in all relevant proceedings, and to be assured a meaningful opportunity to observe, and take part in, all such proceedings. These are the very kinds of rights with which our Constitution is typically and properly concerned. Specifically, our Constitution's central concerns involve protecting the rights of individuals to participate in all those government processes that directly and immediately involve those individuals and affect their lives in some focused and particular way. Such rights include the right to vote on an equal basis whenever a matter is put to the electorate for resolution by voting; the right to be heard as a matter of procedural due process when government deprives one of life, liberty, or property; and various rights of the criminally accused to a speedy and public trial, with the assistance of counsel, and with various other participatory safeguards including the right to compulsory process and to confrontation of adverse witnesses. The parallel rights of victims to participate in these proceedings are no less basic, even though they find no parallel recognition in the explicit text of the U.S. Constitution.

An Illustrative Case

Courts have sometimes recognized that the Constitution's failure to say anything explicit about the right of the victim or the victim's family to observe the trial of the accused should not be construed to deny the existence of such a right—provided, of course, that it can be respected consistent with the fair-trial rights of the accused. In *Richmond Newspapers v. Virginia*, 448 U.S. 555 (1980), for example, the plurality opinion, written by Chief Justice [Warren] Burger, noted the way in which protecting the right of the press and the public to attend a criminal trial—even where, as in that case, the accused and the prosecution and the trial judge all preferred a closed proceeding—serves to protect not only random members of the public but those with a more specific interest in observing, and right to observe—namely, the dead victim's close relatives. As Chief Justice Burger wrote, "Civilized societies withdraw both from the victim and the vigilante the enforcement of criminal laws, but they cannot erase from people's

Asay. © 1998 by The Creators Syndicate, Inc. Reprinted with permission.

consciousness the fundamental, natural yearning to see justice done—or even the urge for retribution." Although the Sixth Amendment right to a public trial was held inapplicable in *Richmond Newspapers* on the basis that the Sixth Amendment secures that right only to the accused, and although the First Amendment right to free speech was thought by some to have no direct bearing in the absence of anything like government censorship, the plurality took note of the Ninth Amendment, whose reminder that the Constitution's enumeration of explicit rights is not to be deemed exclusive furnished an additional ground for the plurality's conclusion that the Constitution presupposed, even though it nowhere enumerated, a presumptive right of openness and participation in trial proceedings. Wrote Chief Justice Burger: "Madison's efforts, culminating in the Ninth Amendment, served to allay the fears of those who were concerned that expressing certain guarantees could be read as excluding others."

I discuss *Richmond Newspapers* in some detail here not just because I argued that case but because it illustrates so forcefully the way in which victims' rights to observe and to participate, subject only to such exclusions and regulations as are genuinely essential to the protection of the rights of the accused, may be trampled upon in the course of law enforcement simply out of a concern with administrative convenience or out of an unthinking assumption that, because the Constitution nowhere refers to the rights of victims in so many words, such rights may and perhaps even should be ignored or at least downgraded. The happy coincidence that the rights of the victims in the *Richmond Newspapers* case overlapped with the First Amendment rights of the press prevented the victims in that case—the relatives of a hotel manager who had been found stabbed to death—from being altogether ignored on that occasion. But many victims have no such luck, and there appears to be a considerable body of evidence showing that, even where statutory or regulatory or judge-made rules exist to protect the participatory rights of victims, such rights often tend to be honored in the breach, *not* on the entirely understandable basis of a particularized determination that affording the victim the specific right claimed would demonstrably violate some constitutional right of the accused or convicted offender, but on the very different basis of a barely-considered reflex that protecting a victim's rights would represent either a luxury we cannot afford or a compromise with an ignoble desire for vengeance.

As long as we do so in a manner that respects the separation and division of powers and does not invite judges to interfere with law enforcement resource allocation decisions properly belonging to the political branches, we should not hesitate to make explicit in our Constitution the premise that I believe is implicit in that document but that is unlikely to receive full and effective recognition unless it is brought to the fore and chiseled in constitutional stone—the premise that the processes for enforcing state and federal criminal law must, to the extent possible, be conducted in a manner that respects not only the rights of those accused of having committed a crime but also the rights of those they are accused of having victimized.

Writing an Effective Amendment

The fact that the states and Congress, within their respective jurisdictions, already have ample affirmative authority to enact rules protecting these rights is a reason for not including new *enabling* or *empowering* language in a constitutional amendment on this subject, but is not a reason for opposing an amendment altogether. For the problem with rules enacted in the absence of such a constitutional amendment is not that such rules, assuming they are enacted with care, would be struck down as falling outside the affirmative authority of the relevant jurisdiction. The problem, rather, is that such rules are likely, as experience to date sadly shows, to provide too little real protection whenever they come into conflict with bureaucratic habit, traditional indifference, sheer inertia, or any mention of an accused's rights regardless of whether those rights are genuinely threatened.

Of course any new constitutional language in this area must be drafted so that the rights of victims will not become an excuse for running roughshod over the rights of the accused. Any constitutional amendment in this field must be written so that courts will retain ultimate responsibility for harmonizing, or balancing, the potentially conflicting rights of all participants in any given case. But assuring that this fine-tuning of conflicting rights remains a task for the judiciary should not be too difficult. What is difficult, and perhaps impossible, is assuring that, under the existing system of rights and rules, the constitutional rights of victims— rights that the Framers of the Constitution undoubtedly assumed would receive fuller protection than has proven to be the case—will not instead receive short shrift.

To redress this imbalance, and to do so without distorting the Constitution's essential design, it may well be necessary to add a corrective amendment on this subject. Doing so would neither extend the Constitution to a purely policy issue, nor provide special benefits to a particular interest group, nor use the heavy artillery of constitutional amendment where a less radical solution is available. Nor would it put the Constitution to a merely symbolic use, or enlist it for some narrow or partisan purpose. It would instead, if the provision were properly drafted, help solve a distinct and significant gap in our existing legal system's arrangements for the protection of basic human rights against an important category of governmental abuse.

> *"Crime victims . . . should not be imbued with constitutional rights equivalent to the rights of defendants."*

Crime Victims Do Not Need a Constitutional Amendment

Wendy Kaminer

In the following viewpoint, Wendy Kaminer claims that a victims' rights amendment is impractical and threatens the rights of defendants. She argues that such an amendment would create numerous problems for prosecutors. In addition, Kaminer argues that the real motive of many supporters of victims' rights is to decrease the rights of defendants and their ability to receive a fair trial. Kaminer is a lawyer, author, and senior correspondent for the *American Prospect*.

As you read, consider the following questions:

1. In what ways will giving constitutional rights to crime victims impair prosecutions, in Kaminer's opinion?
2. Why does the author believe victims should not be given rights equivalent to those of the defendants?
3. According to Kaminer, what does it mean to take the presumption of innocence seriously?

From "Victims Versus Suspects," by Wendy Kaminer, *The American Prospect*, March 13, 2000. Copyright © 2000 by The American Prospect, Inc. Reprinted with permission.

In the 1960s, the Supreme Court recognized that people accused of crimes were imbued with constitutional rights, which the states were obliged to respect. In the course of a few years, the Warren Court applied the exclusionary rule to the states, prohibiting the introduction of evidence seized in violation of the Fourth Amendment; it fashioned the Miranda warnings to protect the Fifth Amendment right to remain silent and prevent coerced confessions; it required prosecutors to disclose exculpatory evidence; and it held that states must provide indigent defendants with lawyers at both the trial and appellate levels.

These rulings are commonly and stupidly derided for elevating legal technicalities over questions of guilt: With the exception of the exclusionary rule (which is quite flexible and all too easily avoided), these "technicalities" focus precisely on the question of guilt. Coerced confessions are inherently unreliable; prosecutorial misconduct, like failure to disclose evidence exonerating the defendant, leads to wrongful convictions, as does the denial of competent counsel to poor defendants.

But ensuring the integrity of the trial process has never been a high political priority. Legislators and judges intent on being perceived as "tough on crime" pass laws or issue rulings that increase the likelihood of conviction but not the reliability. Indeed, some rules, like those limiting federal appeals of state court convictions, facilitate unreliable convictions— convictions of innocent people or defendants whose guilt was never proven. Few voters seem to care. The reforms demanded by the Warren Court were undermined by Richard Nixon's law-and-order campaign of the late 1960s, the ongoing war on drugs, and a widespread tendency to presume the guilt of people prosecuted for crimes. In a different world, the Warren Court decisions could have inspired increased respect for the rights of criminal suspects; instead they helped spark a movement to create countervailing rights for crime victims.

Pros and Cons of Victims' Rights

In the past 30 years, the victims' rights movement has generated some welcome reforms, notably the extension of services to crime victims in localities across the country and the renewed prosecutorial attention to victims' concerns. In addition, all the states have adopted legislation or constitutional amendments recognizing the interests of victims in criminal proceedings. Still, Congress is anxious to declare its allegiance to crime victims, partly to affirm its abhorrence of criminal suspects. So for several years the Senate has been threatening to pass the crime victims' rights amendment to the Constitution. It would give victims of violent crimes a right to be present at all public proceedings, a right to be heard regarding negotiated pleas and release from custody, a right to consideration of their interest in a trial "free from unreasonable delay," and a right to restitution from the convicted offender.

What's wrong with these rights? Putting principle aside, for the moment, consider the practicalities: Offering federal constitutional rights to crime victims will greatly complicate and impair prosecutions, which is why the victims' rights amendment has encountered opposition from some prosecutors (including a federal prosecutor in the Oklahoma City bombing case). Granting crime victims vaguely defined rights to speedy trials may pressure prosecutors into trying cases before they are ready; requiring victims to be present during all trial proceedings will often conflict with the need to sequester witnesses since the victims of crime often testify against their alleged attackers; mandating that victims be heard on plea negotiations may lead to delays and possibly more trials (and perhaps fewer convictions since delay often benefits the defendant). Problems like these will be exacerbated in cases involving multiple victims, with multiple prosecutorial agendas of their own. What's a prosecutor to do if one victim urges him to negotiate a plea and another demands that he proceed to trial?

An Attack on Defendants' Rights

The practical problems posed by the victims' rights amendment are, however, less daunting than its repressive ideology. It attacks the presumption of innocence. When we identify and legally empower a victim before conviction, we assume that a crime has been committed, although that is sometimes disputed at trial (think of an acquaintance rape case); we also assume the veracity and reliability of the self-proclaimed victim. It's worth noting that the victims' rights amendment is opposed by many feminist advocates for battered women (including the NOW Legal Defense and Education Fund) because in cases involving domestic violence, the identity of the victim is not always clear. Women who strike back against their abusers are sometimes prosecuted and offer claims of self-defense: These women should not "lose their 'victim' status once they have defended their lives and become defendants," the National Clearinghouse for the Defense of Battered Women asserts. It argues that additional time, money, and energy devoted to helping crime victims should be used to increase support and services for victims outside the courtroom, not to invent questionable constitutional rights within it.

Defining Victims

Among the many people affected by such crimes as racketeering, drug deals, bombings or toxic discharges, who qualifies as a "victim"? Who is a victim of election fraud, or espionage, or obstruction of justice? What does it mean to "exclude" a victim from a proceeding?

Scott Wallace, *Corrections Today*, April 1997.

But victims' rights advocates tend to perceive the rights of defendants and the interests of victims as elements in a zero-sum game. Many don't simply want to increase victim services; they want to decrease defendants' rights and reorient criminal trials so that the victim, not the defendant, occupies center stage. "How might serious crimes . . . be resolved differently if the victims, rather than the offenders, were the center of attention?" Judith Herman asked rhetorically in a recent issue of *The American Prospect* ["Just Dignity," January 31, 2000]. "What if the courtroom drama were a dialogue between the victim and the community about restitution rather than a duel between the prosecution and the defense about punishment?"

Questions like these presume the defendant's guilt. The prosecutor and defense are not engaged in a "duel about punishment"; they're engaged in a duel about guilt. Should we determine the restitution owed by the defendant to the victim before we have determined her guilt? What if the victim is lying or mistaken about the identity of the defendant? (Eyewitness identifications, for example, are notoriously unreliable.) What if police falsify evidence against the defendant; what if the prosecutor has concealed evidence of the defendant's innocence?

Defendants occupy the center of attention in criminal trials because they're the ones being prosecuted. The rights conferred upon criminal suspects are limitations on the power of the state to kill or imprison its citizens. The Bill of Rights reflects the founders' belief that government could not be trusted to exercise its police powers fairly. It reflects the understanding that power is easily abused and that individuals cannot protect themselves against the state without rights that prosecutors are required to respect.

Therapy Versus Justice

Crime victims have a strong moral claim to be treated with respect and compassion, of course; but they should not be imbued with constitutional rights equivalent to the rights of defendants (their liberty and their lives are not at stake), and they should not expect their need to be "healed" or "made whole" by the trial to take precedence over the defendant's right to dispute allegations of guilt. Once guilt has been adjudicated, victims have an appropriate role in sentencing, but even then, courts concerned with equal justice have to guard against letting bias for or against the victim determine punishment. We should, for example, be wary of victim impact statements, which describe the effects of a crime on the victim or the victim's family. These statements can easily favor defendants whose victims lack family or friends to speak for them. The bias they introduce into the sentencing process is especially troubling in capital cases. Should killing a homeless, friendless person be less of a crime than killing someone well-loved by his family and community?

Victims' rights advocates generally view therapy for the victim as a primary form of justice, but in the criminal courts, the demands of therapy and justice conflict. Some crime victims, for example, may find cross-examination traumatic, but it is essential to the defense—and to the search for truth. The victim's credibility must be tested; inaccuracies or inconsistencies in her story must be revealed. Taking a cue from the therapeutic culture, victims' rights advocates tend to impute virtue to victimhood, but, of course, it is sometimes misplaced. Taking the presumption of innocence seriously means that we can never take an accusation at face value.

It's hard to argue with the desire to reform trials in order to help victims heal—unless you consider the consequences. Because the victims' rights amendment decreases the rights of defendants, it's not simply a grant of rights to crime victims; it's a grant of power to the state. Victims need and deserve services, but with nearly two million people already behind bars, the state needs no more power to imprison us.

Periodical Bibliography

The following articles have been selected to supplement the diverse views presented in this chapter.

Gene Callahan and William Anderson	"The Roots of Racial Profiling," *Reason*, August/September 2001.
David Cole	"The Color of Justice," *Nation*, October 11, 1999.
Anne M. Coughlin	"Why Miranda Is Suspect," *Washington Post National Weekly Edition*, December 20–27, 1999.
John J. DiIulio Jr.	"Against Mandatory Minimums," *National Review*, May 17, 1999.
Barbara Dority	"The U.S. Criminal Injustice System," *Humanist*, May 2000.
Samuel Francis	"Miranda Threatens Constitution, Not the Cops," *Conservative Chronicle*, July 12, 2000.
Jeffrey Goldberg	"The Color of Suspicion," *New York Times Magazine*, June 20, 1999.
Orrin G. Hatch	"Miranda Warnings and Voluntary Confessions Can Co-Exist," *Wall Street Journal*, December 13, 1999.
Issues and Controversies on File	"Miranda Warnings," February 18, 2000.
Jon Kyl	"A New Definition of Justice That Includes the Victim," *Corrections Today*, April 1997.
Alexandra Marks	"Black and White View of Police," *Christian Science Monitor*, June 1, 1999.
Alexander Nguyen	"The Assault on Miranda," *American Prospect*, March 27/April 10, 2000.
Jerome H. Skolnick	"The Color of the Law," *American Prospect*, July/August 1998.
Reginald Stuart	"Justice Denied," *Emerge*, May 1998.
Stuart Taylor Jr.	"Should the Supreme Court Dump the Miranda Rules?" *National Journal*, October 23, 1999.
Scott Wallace	"Victims' Rights: Fine but Not in the Constitution," *Corrections Today*, April 1997.

CHAPTER 4

What Should Be the Role of the Media in the Legal System?

Chapter Preface

On December 1, 2000, the American television-viewing public was granted unusual access to the U.S. Supreme Court. On that day, the Court heard arguments on the validity of Florida's presidential election results. Within fifteen minutes of the hearing's conclusion, audiotaped transcripts were made available to the networks. Using pictures of the justices as a visual accompaniment, television was able to bring the highest court in the land to an audience of millions. The decision departed greatly from other Supreme Court cases, in which the audio transcript is not available until several weeks after the arguments had concluded.

Many commentators argue that releasing audiotapes is inadequate and that the Supreme Court should allow television cameras. The Court, however, has been reluctant. Justice David Souter once declared, "The day you see a camera coming into our courtroom, it's going to roll over my dead body." His opinion contrasts sharply with that of the American public. Polls have found that 73 percent of Americans believe they should have television access to the Supreme Court.

In an editorial, the *Los Angeles Times* criticized the Court's refusal to allow cameras: "[The high court's] worry is that cameras would disrupt court decorum and tempt lawyers into displays of grandiloquence, even histrionics. But the experience in state courts, most of which permit cameras, greatly undermines those fears." The paper's position is supported by a study on the effects of cameras in twenty-four states. The only state that reported that the cameras altered the behavior of those in the courtroom was Virginia.

Columnist Nat Hentoff has argued that television access is necessary because the print and broadcast media provide limited information on the Court's decisions. He suggests that the Supreme Court justices "[are] in contempt of the people's right to know about who they are and what they do."

The relationship between the media and the legal system is not limited to the courtroom. In the following chapter, the authors consider the role that the media should play in the legal system.

"[Public viewing of trials] is an unparalleled way to inform the public about vital issues of governance and everyday life."

Cameras Should Be Permitted in Courtrooms

Fred Graham

In the following viewpoint, Fred Graham contends that despite the views of some judges, the public benefits when cameras are permitted in courtrooms. According to Graham, the resistance of judges to allow for the televising of trials is self-contradictory and runs counter to the public interest. He also maintains that courtroom cameras do not adversely affect the behavior of jurors or other trial participants. Instead, Graham argues, public viewing of trials ensures that proceedings are conducted fairly and informs Americans about important issues. Graham is the chief anchor and managing editor of Court TV.

As you read, consider the following questions:

1. Why does Graham believe that banning cameras from courtrooms runs counter to the public interest?
2. According to the author, how were courtrooms set up in early America?
3. According to Graham, what two things must happen in order to best serve the public?

Excerpted from "Doing Justice with Cameras in the Courts," by Fred Graham, *Media Studies Journal*, Winter 1998. Copyright © 1998 by Media Studies Center and The Freedom Forum. Reprinted with permission.

For advocates of cameras in courts, an unfunny thing happened on the way to the millennium—the televised O.J. Simpson trial.

In the early years of the 1990s, television coverage of trials expanded rapidly. The concerns of some lawyers and judges that cameras would adversely affect trials were rarely borne out in the growing number of cases that were televised, and it appeared that the camera had made its case.

A Stalled Experiment

But within two years of the debacle in Judge Lance Ito's courtroom, the rush to televised judgment had stalled. The federal courts, after a successful three-year experiment with TV in court, had rejected camera coverage. California and New York had backed away from their earlier full acceptance of cameras in courts. And virtually without exception, judges across the country presiding over important cases rejected TV coverage of those trials.

Another example of killing the messenger that brought unpleasant news? Partly, yes. But there is more to it than that. It does seem that some of the public repugnance over the unseemly Simpson trial has been turned against the courtroom camera that was a link in the multimedia extravaganza that took place. But beyond that, it now appears that a fundamental unresolved issue about the role of the courts had been festering beneath the surface of the cameras-in-courts debate, one that is being forced into the open by the Simpson backlash.

That issue is, How much importance should the judicial system give to doing justice in public? Is the sole function of the courts to dispense justice between competing parties, so that any proposed measures to inform the public should be rejected if they might conceivably affect a trial? Or is opening the courts to the public a value in itself, which should be accommodated unless there is some showing that the quality of justice would be diminished? . . .

The Simpson Backlash

By the early 1990s, almost every state allowed cameras in some judicial proceedings, and about two-thirds of the states permitted cameras freely into trial courts, subject to the judges' discretion. Some trial judges never allowed them, but that number was dwindling.

Then, in 1995, came the O.J. Simpson trial, followed by a "Simpson backlash" that had a curious impact on thinking within the judiciary.

There's a story about a rooster who crowed at dawn each day and came to believe he made the sun come up. The rooster had it backward, of course, and that's what happened to the judges who concluded that because a television camera was present in Judge Ito's unruly courtroom, it caused the disarray of the Simpson trial. A more logical conclusion would have been that Judge Ito lost control of his courtroom, and the camera permitted the world to see the ugly spectacle that resulted.

As time has passed since the Simpson debacle, it has become apparent that the judiciary is getting something else backward—judges are concluding that because the Simpson trial was a high-profile case, TV cameras should be banned from other high-interest trials.

Understanding Judicial Thinking

This is not just wrongheaded—it's counter to the public interest.

It seems to be fostering a new judicial assumption that if a trial is interesting to the public, by definition it is one they should not be permitted to see. The result could be that the trials most likely to inform the American people about matters of public importance will not be available to them.

How did judicial thinking on cameras in courts become so self-contradictory?

The process began when Los Angeles Superior Court Judge Hiroshi Fujisaki banned cameras from the O.J. Simpson civil trial, and then, in his usual firm manner, conducted a dignified trial.

In hindsight, it is obvious that the elements that made the Ito trial a shambles were absent from the civil case. The raucous race issue was kept out of the trial; the lawyers were professional and restrained; and Judge Fujisaki demonstrated that he would have run a proper trial under any circumstances. It seems likely that if Judge Fujisaki had permitted camera coverage, the trial would have proceeded in a decorous manner, and the "Simpson backlash" against cameras would have ended there.

Banning Cameras Undermines the Public

"In an age when most people learn about public affairs from television, courts cannot really be described as open if cameras are excluded. Robert Barton, a long-serving Associate Justice of the Massachusetts Superior Court says that 'The bottom line is that the courts belong to the public. They don't belong to the judge, the lawyers or the litigants. The public has a right to know.'

"It is a blanket ban on courtroom cameras which undermines the public's faith in any country's justice system, not their presence. Instead of seeing what actually goes on in courtrooms, people are left to rely on the wildly inaccurate and melodramatic fictional depictions in films and television shows. For example, they are misled into thinking that lawyers endlessly interrupt each other. . . . People with experience of real courts know that such dramatic flourishes are unacceptable. They are also misled into thinking that crime, which is extensively reported by television in every country, is rarely punished, because the public does not get to see the trials of those charged with a crime."

Economist, December 19, 1998.

But as it happened, after the debacle of the first Simpson trial, virtually every judge presiding over a high-visibility trial found some reason to ban cameras. It happened in the South Carolina child-drowning trial of Susan Smith; in the Texas trial of the accused killer of singing star Selena; in the New Jersey child-murder trial of Jesse Timmendequas, whose crime inspired "Megan's law"; in the California murder trial of Richard Allen Davis, whose murder of Polly Klaas inspired the "three strikes you're out" laws; and even in the second trial of the Menendez brothers.

None of these judges gave an up-front rationale that they were banning TV coverage because there was high public interest in the trial. But by mid-1997, the pattern was so well established that essentially that reason was given by the judge who banned cameras from the trial of the Pakistani man accused of killing two CIA employees outside the agency's Langley, Va., headquarters. "It is the very high-profile nature of this case," Judge J. Howe Brown explained, "that makes it unique and makes cameras inappropriate."

Finally, the untelevised Timothy McVeigh bombing trial, conducted by Federal District Judge Richard Matsch with efficiency and dignity, seemed to authenticate the growing judicial notion that important trials shouldn't be on TV.

The Fears of Judges

The irony is that almost all of the 47 states that allow camera coverage of court proceedings first conducted an experiment or study showing that cameras are not harmful, and those findings are still valid. Some included detailed studies indicating that cameras did not adversely affect the behavior of judges, attorneys and others. Yet with no empirical evidence to alter those findings, judges are carving out a "high-profile" exception to the laws allowing cameras in court.

The most frequent reason given is that televising high-interest cases may upset witnesses or jurors. But there's no evidence that anybody who would be unnerved by a camera wouldn't be equally unstrung by the intensity of a major case with the courtroom crammed with print reporters and the cameras waiting outside.

In fact, no coherent rationale has been given for creating a "high-profile" exemption, and cameras are allowed in routine cases as fully as ever.

Why is this happening?

With some judges, the real motivation for barring cameras from big cases may be "Itophobia"—fear of appearing as inept as Judge Ito, with the multitudes watching. Others genuinely believe that the misbehavior of the lawyers in the Simpson case was stimulated by the cameras—not by Judge Ito's lack of control—and that high-profile cases encourage lawyers to showboat. Some judges and lawyers are also horrified that another widely watched televised trial might again show the public the system's warts, writ large, as in the Simpson case.

There is also a subtle sentiment among some judges that

allowing themselves to be seen on television is injudicious and unseemly, even if it doesn't harm the trial. The unspoken corollary of this mindset is that those judges who do permit cameras are, perhaps, show-offs.

This feeling is quietly nourished by the example of the U.S. Supreme Court—which refuses to permit TV coverage of its proceedings, even though this would be immensely instructive to the American public and couldn't possibly affect the outcome of any case. The justices have never been moved to give their reasons for refusing, but stray comments by a few justices suggest that they do not wish to be recognized in public, and they fear that being seen on TV might diminish the lofty mystique of the Court.

This mindset may be the core of the problem. Some judges appear to place no value on the opportunity for the public to see justice in progress—so that any countervailing factor, however questionable and speculative, tips the scales toward banning TV coverage.

The Importance of Public Viewing

Too many judges seem almost oblivious to the long tradition of public viewing of trials in America, and to the powerful reasons for it. Our nation inherited the tradition from England, where in the 16th century all the townspeople were actually required to attend trials, and later, when that proved a burden, the rule was relaxed and all were encouraged to attend. In that spirit, the early American courtrooms were huge, theaterlike set-ups where, as Justice Holmes put it, "every citizen should be able to satisfy himself with his own eyes" that justice was being conducted fairly. Thus the reason for the tradition of public viewing was to validate the judicial system itself. As Chief Justice Warren Burger put it, this openness was "an indispensable attribute of an Anglo-American trial," because it "gave assurance that the proceedings were conducted fairly to all concerned, and it discouraged perjury, the misconduct of participants, and decisions based on secret bias or partiality."

But in modern America, there are additional reasons for public viewing of trials: It is an unparalleled way to inform the public about vital issues of governance and everyday life.

Present-day Americans are often isolated and poorly informed about their government and their neighbors. Much of what they know they get from television.

For instance, people could learn valuable lessons from viewing the trial of accused Langley killer Mir Aimal Kansi. Why was he so embittered against the CIA? Was the agency's security adequate? Did the government violate his rights in bringing him back for trial? Even if so, was it justified?

Consider what millions of Americans might have learned from watching the Oklahoma City bombing trial on television: In human terms, the story was told of young men's resentment of the powerful government, their outrage over the Waco, Texas, killings, their paranoia, their lack of moral restraint and the capacity of a very few of them to do great harm.

Witness middle-profile trials that were televised, despite the Simpson backlash: the latest assisted-suicide trial of Dr. Jack Kevorkian and the case of two Army skinheads from Fort Bragg, N.C., accused of the racist murders of two blacks. The Kevorkian trial exposed serious questions as to whether the woman who committed suicide might have felt improper family pressures to do so. The skinhead trial revealed an astonishing ignorance by the Army of racist (and, by the way, sexual) activity in its barracks. . . .

How to Best Serve the Public

It is apparent that the public will be best served when two things happen: When the nation's judges exercise the courage and public spirit to admit cameras to the trials—and when broadcasters present the trials in a manner that responsibly informs the viewers. Then, both the judiciary and the television medium will genuinely have something to crow about.

"To expect judicious (so to say) coverage of trials and civil suits . . . is to expect too much."

Cameras Should Not Be Allowed in Courtrooms

Woody West

In the following viewpoint, Woody West argues that placing cameras in courtrooms will not improve coverage of the legal system or reduce judicial activism. According to West, television coverage is likely to remain focused on drama instead of substance. He also asserts that despite the claims of some conservatives, "demystifying" the courts by allowing for the greater use of cameras is more likely to degrade the judicial system than reduce activism by liberal judges. West is an associate editor for *Insight on the News*.

As you read, consider the following questions:
1. What is the "demystifying" argument in favor of cameras in the courtroom, as defined by the author?
2. In the author's opinion, what type of trial scenes does television show most frequently?
3. What is West's response to the suggestion that television can help reduce judicial legislating?

There are times when it is essential simply to stand in the road and shout, "Stop!" So counseled William F. Buckley Jr. years ago. Though conservatism now has become almost respectable, there are times when that tactic still has visceral appeal—for instance, when it comes to infesting more U.S. courtrooms with television cameras.

It is the case, however, that those dreaded video devices have penetrated nearly every crevice of the republic by now. State and local courtrooms by and large have acceded to their presence. The principal institutional holdout is the federal judiciary.

Arguments for Courtroom Televisions

There is sentiment to pierce that veil as well to include the Supreme Court in the broadcasting. Perhaps we eventually will get it—like measles or the chicken pox.

Disconcertingly, some on the right sanction the expansion. The argument is that "demystifying" the courts would expose the liberal-left activists on the bench. This, the reasoning goes, would make the public aware of culturally destructive rulings as they come to us case by case.

Another argument is that extending courtroom television would make unnecessary other measures that have been proposed to corral judicial activism. One of these is for Congress vigorously to impeach federal judges too frisky in their leftist enthusiasms. Viscerally appealing as that might be, it would take greater political audacity than congressional Republicans are demonstrating in the present shy-maiden mode.

Thus this advocacy for widening television's presence. The position forcefully was expressed, though not quite convincingly, by a Washington lawyer in an op-ed column in the *Washington Times*. Daniel E. Troy began by borrowing Robert Bork's phrase concerning the necessity for demystifying the courts and then offered as a premise that "video is our society's common language"—which is too true to be good.

Liberals view the judiciary as the vehicle of last resort through which they can achieve their political agenda, he contends, while publicly extolling the courts as the sole defenders of individual liberties. No argument there. "Televising federal court proceedings is vital if that myth is ever to be punctured. . . ."

But for those who blanch at the notion that television can puncture anything other than good taste and a resistant attention span, that's a drafty thesis.

Questioning the Public's Right to Know

Much as I would like to argue, as many television stations do, that covering courtroom trials is a news event, I remain unconvinced. What, for instance, was especially newsworthy about the Simpson trials? Apart from the entering of a plea, the opening arguments, some testimony and, of course, the verdicts, what was so important about the Simpson case to warrant the type of continuing massive live media exposure that so many journalists were willing to give it?

Although many media lawyers might reflectively argue that the public has a right to know what was happening live in Judge Ito's courtroom, as it happens, I'm not sure that in a case such as Simpson's we should be invoking a first amendment mantra reserved for monitoring the actions of government or debates over political policy. Indeed, if the public's right to know was the true motivation for coverage, why did CNN and other television stations interrupt the live satellite feed of the proceedings with frequent commercials?

Michael M. Epstein, *Television Quarterly*, vol. 28, no. 4, 1997.

The op-ed barrister argues that 48 states now permit courtroom cameras and the "empirical data" does not substantiate concern that cameras adversely affect behavior at trials. Never mind that "empirical data" cannot be extracted from a nonempirical context—that is, from the strata of emotion and anxiety that swirl in a courtroom. No matter how many social scientists dance their methodological tango, there is no valid way to demonstrate that television in the court does or does not affect the way the drama unfolds.

Nevertheless, anyone who ever snapped a Kodak Brownie knows that any camera changes that upon which it focuses, from family picnic to Rose Garden gala. Except in the hands of an occasional genius, pictures only are provisionally accurate and even less so when those behind the camera attempt to convey the profound rituals of a culture.

The op-ed essayist also believes television cameras would

"enable television journalists to cover the federal courts more aggressively." But in the real world, television trial snippets routinely are of a weeping victim, a sullen defendant or a searing confrontation, lasting about 25 seconds. There is, moreover, nothing that now impedes television from reporting the significance of a judicial proceeding if television nabobs are willing to emphasize substance over dramatic froth.

Degrading the Court System

But take the broader contention of the usefulness of demystifying institutions, as Bork emphasizes. After the nasty ordeal he was subjected to, it would be understandable if Bork wished not only to demystify but to raze the law schools and sow salt where they stood. But note that the essayist then wheels out a supporting cast that includes such luminaries of the left as Democratic Reps. Barney Frank of Massachusetts, Charlie Schumer of New York and Ron Dellums of California.

To suppose that they advocate cameras in federal courtrooms to expose liberal activism is a stunning proposition. The logical likelihood is that the liberals who would "demystify" the court system are, rather, intent on stripping from it the majesty that must be part of the dignity of humane institutions. To reduce the legal edifice that was hard generations in creation to another televised spectacle is to degrade it further.

Television has its virtues, as exemplified by C-Span and occasionally by the commercial networks. To expect judicious (so to say) coverage of trials and civil suits, though, is to expect too much. A pup piddles because it is a pup.

Curtailing judicial activism only will occur as presidents who oppose it make appropriate appointments to the federal bench. There's no quick fix. To suggest that television can assist in reducing judicial legislating is like Dr. Johnson's definition of a second marriage as a triumph of hope over experience.

So: Stop!

> "Such an extreme exercise of the public will
> and the state's power demands a public
> witness."

Timothy McVeigh's Execution Should Have Been Televised

Thomas Lynch

Televising executions, such as that of Oklahoma City bomber Timothy McVeigh, will force people to confront the reality of the death penalty, Thomas Lynch argues in the following viewpoint. He contends that the public must bear witness when a government exercises its power to kill. Lynch asserts that showing executions on television will not turn those events into spectacles but will instead enable Americans to decide the real purpose of the death penalty. This viewpoint was written prior to the McVeigh's execution. Although McVeigh's request to have his death televised was denied, Attorney General John Ashcroft did allow the families of McVeigh's victims to watch the execution on closed-circuit television. Lynch is a funeral director and author.

As you read, consider the following questions:

1. According to Lynch, why are cameras sent when the United States bombs another country?
2. Why does the author believe that televising Timothy McVeigh's execution will not turn McVeigh into a martyr?
3. How did viewing the assisted suicide of one of Jack Kevorkian's patients change public opinion of such deaths, in Lynch's view?

From "Witness and Remember," by Thomas Lynch, *Christian Century*, May 21, 2001. Copyright © 2001 by The Christian Century Foundation. Reprinted with permission.

After 30 years of directing funerals, I've come to believe in open caskets. A service to which everybody but the deceased is invited, like a wedding without the bride or a baptism without the baby, denies the essential reality of the occasion, misses the focal point. It is why we comb wreckage, drag rivers and bring our war dead home. Knowing is better than not knowing, no matter how difficult the facts; and seeing, it turns out, is believing. That's what hurts, the heart-sore widow says of the body in the blue suit in the box. Births, deaths, marriages—the fashions of these passages change, but the fundamental obligations of witness and remembrance remain. And whether we bear witness to the joy or sadness, the love or grief, the life or death, the sharing of it makes the bearing of it better.

Confronting Loss and Death

Which is why we searched the devastation in Oklahoma City—to return the bodies of the dead to the families they belonged to. To deal with loss, we must confront our losses. Witness and remembrance are akin.

The same is so for executions. Knowing is better than not knowing. Seeing is believing. Such an extreme exercise of the public will and the state's power demands a public witness.

For people of faith, witness and remembrance are essential stations in their pilgrimage. Passover and Crucifixion, Crusade and Holocaust—these are flesh-and-blood events that call upon the flesh-and-blood faithful to "see and believe," to "watch and not forget." They are not pleasant, but they are compelling. And while Christ chided Thomas for his famous doubt, two millennia later we are glad to have his unambiguous testimony: "My Lord!" he said, changed utterly by the moment, "My God?" We might reasonably wonder if those first Jewish Christians would have embraced the meaning of Christ's execution if Pilate had decided to do it behind closed doors, or if Thomas and his co-religionists had never seen the dead man raised to life.

Scripture and liturgy are the record and replay of what was seen and heard. Nowadays we watch for signs and wonders on TV.

When Timothy McVeigh [was] put to death by lethal injection on May 16, 2001, [the execution was delayed until June 2001] it [was] the first federal execution in nearly 40 years. For most Americans alive today, it [was] the first time in our adult lives that one of our own kind—human kind—[was] capitally punished by the government to which we pledge our allegiance and pay our taxes. And yet, except for a select few, none of us [was] allowed to watch. The suggestion that this execution be televised is dismissed out of hand by the powers that be for reasons never clearly articulated, and in doing so they substantially undermine the rights and duties of citizens in a democracy to scrutinize the exercise of a government's lethal powers.

When we bomb Iraqis or Serbians, when we send troops into harm's way with weapons that kill, we send along the cameras too, because it is our right—some would say our duty—to witness the killing that is done in our names. If that is so in Kosovo, why oughtn't it be so in Indianapolis when a legal, justifiable and state-sanctioned dose of homicide is visited upon the Oklahoma City Bomber on behalf of We the People?

For most of history the public square has been where these things were done—it's the place for politicos and preachers, the sideshows and snake oil, the floggings and the hangings, the public spectacles and entertainments and civic business. The public square is now the TV screen where candidates and con artists, circus and sales pitch, pundits and the evening news all get aired, for all to see. We may choose not to watch, but should we be denied access?

Refuting Arguments Against Televising Executions

So why not public executions?

"Bad taste," it is argued, as if *Temptation Island* or *Jerry Springer* were benchmarks of culture. To be sure, if we only televised what edified, the screen would be blank most hours of most days. That "it might make him a martyr" seems unlikely. A vicious dog put down does not become a much-missed pet. And seeing an evil man put to death will neither add to nor subtract from the terrible math: 19 children, 149 adults—168 innocents murdered by his horrific evil. Those mistaken enough to regard McVeigh as a martyr will not be disabused of their ignorance by his death, seen or unseen. Those who know evil when they see it will not confuse McVeigh with Martin Luther King Jr. or St. Catherine of Sienna. "It might be turned into a spectacle" is another caution, as if the medium cannot distinguish between witness and entertainment, as if the terrorism McVeigh visited upon Oklahoma City and the society at large was not "spectacular." Television does Senate hearings and Super Bowls, the World Wrestling Federation and Book TV. It does not entirely confuse the death of princes or the burial of princesses with *Bowling for Dollars* or *The Dating Game*. It could, quite conceivably, get an execution "fight." But getting it wrong is still better than not getting it at all.

Making People React

One of the primary justifications for the death penalty is that it deters future crime. Since people react to what they see, not what they vaguely imagine, how can we expect to impress would-be felons with an invisible threat? . . .

Perhaps we demand television do the impossible: to make us comfortable in our discomfort. Tough choices cannot be made without a full airing of passionate arguments by each side. For all his ugliness, McVeigh has pulled open the black curtain to reveal a window of opportunity. We could utilize the most powerful communication device ever built to let each one of us decide our best interest. Instead, we will avert our eyes from the silent message behind the blank screen: I don't trust anyone to watch a televised execution for the "right" reason.

Stan Statham, *Vital Speeches of the Day*, July 1, 2001.

Of course, the real concern is that a country that claims to be "for" the death penalty mightn't have the stomach to see exactly what it is that it is "for." Is it possible that the idea of the thing is less disturbing than the thing itself, the abstract more palatable than the actual fact in the way that "a woman's right to choose" is a tidier concept than jars of dead fetuses that look like us? Is it likely that our bravery and braggadocio might wither a little by watching someone put down, more or less like a cocker spaniel or Cheshire cat—not because of what is done to McVeigh, but because of what is done to us?

For years my fellow citizens of Michigan, a state that does not have the death penalty, debated the relative merits of "assisted suicide" while Jack Kevorkian dispatched 120-odd of our fellow citizens, in the name of mercy and kindness and, oh yes, dignity. This was accomplished in the back of an old van with lethal gases and then potassium chloride, and with remarkable impunity. And we acquitted him, every chance we got, persuaded by the rhetoricals of Geoffrey Feiger, his erstwhile advocate, to wit: "If it's good enough for our pets, why not for our parents?" We liked the sound of that and went about our business until one Sunday night in prime time CBS broadcast the snuff film, starring Dr. Jack and Thomas Youk. Once we saw it there on the TV in living color, mercy and dignity looked suspiciously like serial killing. Witness—seeing the thing itself being done—provided a clarity that was missing from the disembodied discussion. Kevorkian got ten to 25 years.

Do Not Look Away from Death

Smug and resolute and unrepentant, Timothy McVeigh is our most evil evildoer. Because he victimized the nation, it is the nation that judges and punishes him. Because his crime was broadcast in real time and in color, the images of the dead and damaged remain vivid in our memories. A child dying in a fireman's arms, the broken and bandaged, the frightened, heartbroken, wounded and lost, the bodies and parts of bodies, the terrible shell of the bombed building—we witnessed these things and we remember. It ought to be easy to watch him die. Still, something in us argues, maybe not. Maybe even a little remedial dose of court-ordered, court-sanctioned homicide, in response to massive evil, kills a little something in ourselves. Maybe we cannot kill others of our kind without risking something of our own humanity.

But the die in McVeigh's case is already cast. And while he has no rights in the matter, we the people certainly do. Surely the value of the death penalty must be measured not only by the difference it makes to the criminal but by the difference it makes to a community of victims in whose name

171

the killer is killed. But whether it soothes or saddens, comforts or vexes, whether it moves us to march against it or to pray, whether we are silenced or sickened by it, is it not our duty to have a look? Would it not tell us something important about ourselves? Whether we are for or against capital punishment, oughtn't citizens of a participatory democracy participate when the will of the people is so profoundly, so irreversibly wrought?

For a generation, we've debated the justice and humanity of existential issues—war, abortion, euthanasia, cloning—the things that have to do with being and ceasing to be. The national dialogue on the death penalty has been carded on by a nation of pundits, commentators, politicos and preachers, policy-makers and coffee-clutch advocates on either side. It is time a nation of opinionizers became a nation of witnesses. It would up the ante on this difficult conversation and bring us that much nearer to a clear view. We cannot declare closure or proclaim justice done. We can only hope to achieve them by confronting our most difficult realities. If we cannot watch, then we should reconsider. We did not look away from the crime. We ought not look away from its punishment.

If what we intend to do to Timothy McVeigh is justice, why wouldn't we watch it? To be a deterrent, shouldn't it be seen? If it is good riddance, sweet revenge, righteousness or humanity—if it is any of these things, why shouldn't we look? If it is none of these things, why do we do it at all?

"*A live TV execution is no more art than a live tornado or car crash.*"

Timothy McVeigh's Execution Should Not Have Been Televised

Raymond A. Schroth

Oklahoma City bomber Timothy McVeigh was executed in June 2001. Prior to his death, McVeigh requested that his execution be televised. Although the request was denied, Attorney General John Ashcroft decided to let families of McVeigh's victims view the proceedings on closed-circuit television. In the following viewpoint, written prior to McVeigh's death, Raymond A. Schroth expresses his disagreement with Ashcroft's decision and argues that executions should not be televised. He asserts that watching such a death diminishes humanity. He concludes that televised executions will seem no more real than a sitcom or any other entertainment. Schroth is the media critic for *National Catholic Reporter*.

As you read, consider the following questions:

1. In Schroth's opinion, what would happen if Timothy McVeigh's request to have his execution televised was granted?
2. According to the author, what happens when a person takes satisfaction from watching someone else die?
3. What does Schroth believe is the difference between reading about an execution and viewing it?

In January 2001 when those who wanted a better attorney general than Missouri's ex-senator John Ashcroft got hold of the videotape of a talk he gave at Bob Jones University, they hoped it would contain a "smoking gun" that would sink—I almost said kill—his nomination.

Alas, there was no smoking gun—merely his proclamation that Jesus is Lord.

Legal Ethics in the Bible

[In April 2001,] on Wednesday of Holy Week, I concluded my night class in the Ethics of Criminal Justice by reading the passion account from the gospel of Luke and let the class draw its own conclusions on how it fit into the course.

Among other things, they saw an innocent man who did not resist arrest. He was framed, tortured and executed to gratify a mob that enjoyed the show.

Timothy McVeigh is no innocent. He is a mass murderer who has been justly tried and convicted. And like every American who is convinced that he has not really lived if he has not had his five minutes on TV, he wants to leave this world with all of us watching. McVeigh's letter proposing a public broadcast of his execution was published in the *Sunday Oklahoman* earlier this year.

Granting his request allows the moral distinction between him and the rest of us to slip away. It makes it look as if we are all just as bloodthirsty as he.

An Embarrassing Decision

In Ashcroft we have a self-proclaimed man of God who is an embarrassment to Christianity. The smoking gun has appeared: It is his decision to literally make a show out of McVeigh's execution, broadcasting it on closed-circuit TV to an invitation-only audience. It would be composed of 250 people from victims' families, along with survivors of the bomb blast that tore apart the federal building in Oklahoma City on April 19, 1995, leaving 168 people dead.

Viewing McVeigh's death, the Christian attorney general believes, will bring "closure" to the grieving.

To no one's surprise, an Internet company, Entertainment Network, Inc., a producer specializing in voyeuristic "reality" viewing, has claimed a First Amendment right to show a pay-per-view live video of the death on its Web site, so you and I may enjoy—excuse me, find closure in—the spectacle. A U.S. district judge was expected to rule April 20, 2001, on the company's request. [The request was denied.]

" WHAT DID YOU EXPECT ?...IT'S SWEEPS WEEK..."

Though most journalism students know the case where the *New York Daily News* photographer strapped a camera to his ankle to secretly snap the electrocution of husband-killer Ruth Snyder in 1928, common decency and the law have long barred cameras from executions. But, as some in criminal justice class said, as we discussed the morality of the death penalty, "Of course they would want to televise McVeigh's death. Everyone would watch it—even though they know it's sick. It follows naturally from *Survivor* and the reality-TV phenomenon it inspired."

So they're running out of material. What do they do next? Execution and death.

Closure? Watching a human being die will make the rest of us feel better? Now the families of victims will miss their loved ones less? No longer haunted by the rubble, smoke and corpses of that day, they will conjure up the image of

McVeigh's dead body and find peace?

We have sometimes found peace in visiting a friend or family member in his or her last hours or minutes. But what brings the peace is our love, the final affirmation of our shared lives. To take satisfaction from watching another human being die, even one who is an enemy, is to diminish, pervert, our own humanity. And it no more purges our grief than a raging scream drains off our anger.

I've read depictions of executions and taught journalists about them, but the closest I've come to watching a killer die was reading my friend Mike Wilson's account in the *Mobile Register* (June 10, 1997) of the electrocution of Henry Francis Hays. Hays had strangled, cut and lynched a 19-year-old black man. The electrocution was not like in the movies, Wilson wrote. As the 2,100 volts shot into him, Hays' body jumped and jerked against the straps "like he was trying to fly."

His "throat turned very red. His thumbs slammed into his fists." For two full minutes the voltage fried his brain and organs until the "lifeless body sagged into the seat."

Young Wilson, who now works in Portland at the *Oregonian*, turned to Hays' brother and to his attorney and embraced them both. If the embrace meant that he would no longer be sent to cover executions, it would be fine with him.

Why is it all right, a student asks, to read about an execution —as in the forthcoming book on McVeigh or in Wilson's story—but not to watch it on TV?

A good question.

Why Watching Is Different from Reading

Because the effect is, to some degree, determined by the medium. The well-written news story is literature. It engages us totally—our imaginations, our moral and critical senses. Yet we control the experience. We put the book down to think, to weep.

Hays, whom I had never heard of before Wilson's articles, became human through Wilson's account. Like the director and film editor of *Dead Man Walking*, the journalist and his editor structure their scenes for effect. Both they and we know that they can degrade us with sensationalism or lead us to affirm life anew.

A live TV execution is no more art than a live tornado or car crash. One moment the prisoner is a curiosity, an entertainer. The next he is a corpse. It is lights and colors in a box in my room, which I watch with one eye on the screen and the other on my email. This will be called "reality."

Because of the way we have been conditioned to watch TV, though, it is just another show, no more reality than a sitcom. Click! Or MTV. Click! Or John Wayne on American Movie Classics. Click!

Or, now this. The evening news next May 16 [following the publication of this viewpoint, McVeigh's execution was postponed until June 2001]: "Timothy McVeigh died today, executed for the Oklahoma City bombing, which killed 168 people, while survivors and victims watched via closed-circuit TV."

"On balance, the mass media offer an inaccurate—or at least incomplete—picture of the daily workings of the criminal courts."

The Media Provide a Poor Understanding of the Legal System

Richard L. Fox and Robert W. Van Sickel

In the following viewpoint, Richard L. Fox and Robert W. Van Sickel claim that television coverage of high-profile trials, such as the O.J. Simpson and Rodney King cases, miseducates the public about the legal system. According to the authors, television coverage overemphasizes the personal and dramatic elements of trials instead of informing its audience about the complexities of the legal system. Fox is an assistant professor of political science at Union College in Schenectady, New York, and Van Sickel is an assistant professor of political science at Purdue University Calumet in Hammond, Indiana. They are the coauthors of *Tabloid Justice: Criminal Justice in an Age of Media Frenzy*, the book from which the following viewpoint has been excerpted.

As you read, consider the following questions:
1. According to Gilbert Geis and Leigh B. Bienen, what have most of the high-profile trials of the twentieth century had in common?
2. What is serialization, as defined by Fox and Van Sickel?
3. In the authors' opinions, what is the effect when important trials are presented in the same fashion as more trivial cases?

Excerpted from *Tabloid Justice: Criminal Justice in an Age of Media Frenzy*, by Richard L. Fox and Robert W. Van Sickel (Boulder, CO: Lynne Rienner, 2001). Copyright © 2001 by Lynne Rienner Publishers. Reprinted with permission.

Historically, U.S. trial courts have been the source of significant media coverage, especially fictionalized stories in both film and print. This attention, however, has always been episodic and often superficial. And though local television news has always devoted significant attention to crime stories, both the public and the mass media have typically ignored everyday trials. For the press to report on a given criminal investigation or trial, there needs to be some factor present that is unusual or out of the ordinary, a prerequisite of newsworthiness identified by both Richard Davis and Herbert Gans, among others. For instance, although hundreds of children in the United States are murdered or abducted each year, the JonBenet Ramsey investigation drew massive attention partly because it involved a six-year-old beauty queen from an extremely wealthy and prominent family.

The Characteristics of Tabloid Justice

In their book *Crimes of the Century*, Gilbert Geis and Leigh B. Bienen assert that many of the high-profile trials in the twentieth century have certain common features, such as the geographic setting of the events, the nature of the offenders and victims, and the details of the offense itself. Crimes that rise to the level of media obsession have tended to occur in the three major media markets of New York (the Charles Lindbergh baby trial, Alger Hiss, Son of Sam, Marv Albert), Chicago (Leopold and Loeb), and Los Angeles (Fatty Arbuckle, Charles Manson, the Rodney King case, O.J. Simpson). However, the increasing news homogenization, engendered by the growth of the Internet and twenty-four-hour cable news, seems to have altered this pattern, as recent tabloid-type cases have originated variously in Miami, Boston, Denver, South Carolina, and Montana.

Criminal cases that receive high volumes of media coverage normally involve provocative or shocking offenses, particularly murder (especially multiple homicides, sexual brutality, or the killing of children), although cases such as that of Alger Hiss (peacetime espionage) and Bill Clinton (perjury and obstruction of justice) do not fit neatly into such categories. As far as the identities of the perpetrators and victims go, the mass media stakes are often raised when the perpetrator is a prominent celebrity or public figure (1920s film star Fatty Arbuckle, William Kennedy Smith, O.J. Simpson, Marv Albert, President Clinton), or when the victim is a particularly unusual, intriguing, or sympathetic personality (Leopold and Loeb's alleged murder of a teenage girl, Louise Woodward's killing of an infant in her care, and JonBenet Ramsey, the six-year-old beauty queen). Sometimes the offender may not have previously been prominent or well-known but comes to represent or illustrate the public's dissatisfaction with particular institutions within the criminal justice system, as in the case of Rodney King and the Los Angeles Police Department (LAPD) and the LAPD again in the Simpson criminal trial.

Top Tabloid Justice Cases of the 1990s

Trial or Investigation	Year the Main Proceeding Concluded
Trial of William Kennedy Smith	1991
Trial of the officers in the Rodney King beating	1992
Trial of Lyle and Erik Menendez	1993
Trial of O.J. Simpson (criminal)	1995
Trial of Louise Woodward	1997
Trial of O.J. Simpson (civil)	1997
Investigation of President Bill Clinton and Monica Lewinsky	1999
Investigation of the murder of JonBenet Ramsey	ongoing

Note: The JonBenet Ramsey investigation began in December 1996.

Richard L. Fox and Robert W. Van Sickel, *Tabloid Justice: Criminal Justice in an Age of Media Frenzy*, 2001.

In any event, we would argue that it is the nature of the media coverage, rather than the circumstances of the particular case, that characterizes the tabloid justice era. The media's emphasis on the extraordinary and sensational fosters a number of public misconceptions and may lead citizens away from considering more important issues such as plea bargaining, courtroom subcultures, attorney and judge interaction, and court bureaucracies. But rather than present these structural and procedural complexities, the media tend to focus on the personal and dramatic aspects of criminal trials and investigations. Plea bargains do not involve the conflict, tension, or visual images that apparently make a story interesting enough to merit significant press attention.

On balance, the mass media offer an inaccurate—or at least incomplete—picture of the daily workings of the criminal courts. This state of affairs is worsened when we recognize that the types of trials that do receive extended coverage are what criminal justice scholar Ray Surette has called "media trials" and what we term tabloid justice cases. Surette effectively characterizes such trials as "court news as miniseries." High-profile media trials are presented largely as sources of high drama and entertainment, as opposed to opportunities to educate and inform the public on the inner workings of the judicial system. They become the foci of intense public exposure and public interest, and ultimately they become part of the lore of popular culture. Many older Americans can recall the names and faces of the trial participants from previous "trials of the century," such as those involving Fatty Arbuckle, Sacco and Vanzetti, Julius and Ethel Rosenberg, Sam Shepherd, Charles Manson, and Patty Hearst.

Combining News and Entertainment

Tabloid justice–type criminal cases, with their potential for drama and pathos, can be seen as the quintessential vehicles for the melding of the previously distinct news and entertainment aspects of the mass media. During the past ten to fifteen years, patterns of development in the news business, . . . have resulted in far more competition for ratings. As the mainstream flagship institutions of the press have sought to maintain their dominance in such a marketplace, they have increasingly tended to present hard news within a structure formerly reserved for entertainment and features. In Surette's words, "fast-paced, dramatic, superficial presentations and simplistic explanations [have become] the norm." William Haltom, in a study of how the press covers judicial actions, refers to this as *dramatized normality*. He hypothesizes that the "news media dramatize abnormal cases until, over time, they have normalized dramatic cases."

The increasing visibility of criminal trials and investigations, when combined with the entertainment-based style in which they are presented, has given such events a symbolic importance far out of proportion with their actual number and objective significance. Because of their prominence, tabloid justice cases have become central to the social construction of "crime and justice reality"—that is, to the formation of public opinion with regard to important legal and political questions. Competing visions of law, justice, and social reality are debated before the citizenry, with greater ramifications than when a very small percentage of the public tunes into a presidential speech or congressional debate.

Further, the fact that television exposes most Americans to such events holds enormous importance for their effect on the public's legal and political attitudes. Television possesses its own set of imperatives, which encourage the repetitive showing of striking images and the presentation of news in short and dramatic segments. Neither of these television-specific characteristics leads to the presentation of legal proceedings in a manner that is conducive to civic education. More important, though, the three characteristics of *serialization, personification,* and *commodification* appear to dominate how the criminal justice system and tabloid trials are covered by television.

The Three Characteristics of Television Coverage

Criminal trials lend themselves to serialization, or the presentation of news as a series of short dramatic events (involving a relatively small number of recurring characters with specific roles) over an extended period of time. Each day's events in a trial or investigation can be presented in a short, simplified, and catchy news segment. As in the trials of O.J. Simpson and the Rodney King officers, the media received assistance from defense attorneys who, in order to influence that day's news coverage, held daily press conferences. On days in which little activity took place in the courtroom, coverage often consisted solely of information disseminated by the lawyers in these cases.

Personification refers to the presentation of events

through a focus on the emotional, personal, human aspects of a story, often at the expense of context, background, structure, and analysis. This is the manner in which television presents virtually all news, but we believe that it is particularly problematic when this style of coverage is used to present images of the judicial process. After all, law is ideally intended to ensure objectivity, procedure, stability, predictability, and equality; the emotional states, biases, and personal backgrounds of the participants are not, in theory, supposed to influence the outcome of criminal investigations and trials. And yet, national newsmagazines reported on such things as the changing hairstyle of O.J. Simpson prosecutor Marcia Clark. In the JonBenet Ramsey investigation, the media reported on the cost of JonBenet's beauty pageant outfits. And in covering the investigation of President Clinton, ABC National News radio reported that Monica Lewinsky had two blueberry pancakes for breakfast the day independent counsel Ken Starr and members of the House of Representatives questioned her. In sum, presenting the legal system through the lens of individual portraits of idiosyncratic participants undermines the educational function of the media.

The commercial imperatives of television also contribute to the commodification of criminal trials, as these events are packaged, promoted, and sold much like any other media program. Coverage in cases such as those of Louise Woodward, O.J. Simpson, and, more recently, the impeachment and trial of President Clinton, serve as evidence. For instance, *E! Entertainment Television*, a cable station that does not even present any hard news programs, offered daily coverage of the Simpson criminal trial, utilizing its normal entertainment anchorpersons. Tabloid programs such as *A Current Affair*, *Hard Copy*, and *Inside Edition* mounted similar efforts. All of the networks and major cable news stations have presented the Clinton-Lewinsky saga much like a dramatic miniseries, often including a musical theme, logo, and graphic introductory material. This aspect of television coverage affects the public's perception of the occasional tabloid justice case that does, in fact, have important legal or political ramifications. Examples drawn from the cases involving Rodney King, as well as the presidential impeachment and

Senate trial, are instructive. But if undeniably important legal events such as these are presented in a fashion identical to the more publicly trivial cases of JonBenet Ramsey, William Kennedy Smith, Marv Albert, and O.J. Simpson, it is not surprising that the public interprets all such events simply as undifferentiated human entertainment pieces, to be viewed or ignored as one pleases.

The decision by consumers whether to follow coverage of the Clinton impeachment and Senate trial simply becomes another in an undifferentiated range of choices, which are not perceived by the viewer as being related to citizenship or the well-being of the nation. Even though such events offer valuable opportunities for public education about the legal and political systems, the mode of media coverage, combined with the public's apparently uncritical reception of that coverage, undermines the opportunity for substantive civic education.

"Trials don't seek the truth but journalism does."

The Media Do Not Prevent Fair Trials

Bruce W. Sanford

Media coverage of highly publicized trials does not prevent those trials from being fair, Bruce W. Sanford contends in the following viewpoint. According to Sanford, fair and impartial juries can be impaneled despite significant pretrial publicity. He also maintains that allowing for a free media during a trial helps the pursuit of truth and benefits the public and criminal defense attorneys. Sanford is a counsel for the Society of Professional Journalists and the author of *Don't Shoot the Messenger: How Our Growing Hatred of the Media Threatens Free Speech for All of Us.*

As you read, consider the following questions:

1. In Sanford's view, what is hypocritical about defense lawyers' complaints about pretrial publicity?
2. According to the author, what is the sole purpose of criminal trials?
3. In the author's opinion, how does the American tradition of openness benefit the public?

From "Pretrial Posturing Defense Attorneys Complain of Leaks, but Play the Publicity Game as Well as Anyone," by Bruce W. Sanford, *Rocky Mountain News*, March 9, 1997. Copyright © 1997 by The E.W. Scripps Co. Reprinted with permission.

Talk shows, editorial columns and Internet home pages have been clobbering the *Dallas Morning News* for publishing information about Timothy McVeigh's supposed confession to the 1995 Oklahoma City bombing.

Defense Lawyers Are Hypocritical

Much of the "piling on" has come from criminal defense lawyers who have complained bitterly about prejudice to McVeigh's Sixth Amendment right to a fair trial. These lions of the defense bar charge that pretrial publicity that reveals inadmissible evidence poisons the prospective jury pool in Denver.

This chorus of whining is not just unadulterated bunk, it's also hypocritical. The criminal defense bar wants it both ways. They huff and puff about the danger to their clients' rights just as they use selective leaks and their own "spin" on pretrial news stories to manipulate the media for their clients' benefit.

After more than 30 years of celebrated criminal trials, we have learned two facts about pretrial publicity that ought to be indisputable:

Publicity Does Not Cause an Unfair Trial

1. Judges can impanel a fair and impartial jury despite massive pretrial publicity.

Believe it or not, average citizens actually keep their sworn oath to decide a criminal case just on the evidence presented in court, not on extraneous noise. Time and time again, famous defendants have won acquittals after a saturation of adverse publicity prior to trial. Former Texas Governor John Connally beat the rap in the Watergate-era "milk-fund" prosecution. Legendary Washington, D.C., Mayor Marion Barry was acquitted of felony charges despite television's repetitive use of the videotape showing him smoking crack cocaine. And need we even mention the O.J. Simpson case?

History tells us that judges can in fact sort out and excuse potential jurors who have been hopelessly handicapped by pretrial publicity. As the United States Supreme Court recognized in a 1976 ruling which broadly prohibited "gag" orders against pretrial coverage by the media, courts have a wide array of techniques available to them to ferret out jurors who are not up to the task. In *Nebraska Press Association vs. Stuart,* the high court wrote:

"Pretrial publicity, even if pervasive and concentrated, cannot be regarded as leading automatically and in every kind of criminal case to an unfair trial."

Pursuing the Truth

2. Trials don't seek the truth but journalism does.

Criminal trials have a singular, express purpose: to ascertain if the evidence can prove guilt beyond a reasonable doubt. If truth emerges, so much the better. But we have all seen instances where truth was a casualty of litigation.

Media Influence Is Overestimated

Legal experts and media lawyers say judges overestimate the influence of news stories on potential jurors, assume that every story is prejudicial, and believe that every candidate for jury duty reads or listens to them all.

"It's a nonissue," said Karl Manheim, professor of constitutional and communications law at Loyola Law School. "What they read in the press is the least important influence on their bias. It's their upbringing and culture, education, their whole persona that will determine their bias."

Most media coverage of court cases consists of routine reports on developments in the case.

When newspapers and television carry pretrial stories that report on evidence or analyze the merits of a case, there are procedures judges can use to find people who were not exposed to those articles or newscasts. Judges can question them very closely to find out precisely what stories they have read or seen and how those stories have influenced them.

Steve Berry, *Los Angeles Times,* May 24, 1998.

Journalism, on the other hand, has as its chief purpose the pursuit of truth. Certainly, most news reports, including the *Dallas Morning News'*, just deal in the currency of accurate facts, not ultimate truth. But at least they aspire in the right direction.

In the 23 months since a bomb exploded in front of the Alfred P. Murrah federal building in Oklahoma City, killing

168 people and injuring another 500, the print and electronic media have pursued thousands of tips. The resulting news reports have compelled McVeigh's lead attorney Stephen Jones to claim that his client could not get a fair trial, and to threaten that he would seek a federal investigation and a delay of the trial. As the case heads toward trial, Jones has used the media for his own purposes, calling into question key prosecution evidence. Yet, when the news isn't favorable, Jones readily telephones reporters to argue that press coverage will taint the jury pool. He also proceeds to muddy the waters by putting out his own spin on the evidence, whether it's admissible or not.

After several days of posturing, Steven Jones has acknowledged that the *Morning News'* story will not jeopardize a fair trial and has agreed that it can start as scheduled on March 31, 1997. Such a concession reiterates the fact that there was no legal justification preventing the *Morning News* from publishing its story.

The logical conclusion to be drawn from the criticism of the press by Jones and other criminal defense attorneys would be adoption of a rule similar to that in England, where the media can report little on court proceedings until a verdict is issued. Such prior restraint, fortunately, is not a part of the American grain. Instead, our traditions of openness benefit both the public—which receives abundant information about its criminal justice system—and criminal defense attorneys, who are increasingly turning their defense of high-profile criminals into lucrative second careers on the speaking and book circuit.

Periodical Bibliography

The following articles have been selected to supplement the diverse views presented in this chapter.

Steve Berry	"When Secrecy Denies the Public's Right to Know," *Los Angeles Times*, May 24, 1998.
Steven Brill	"Cameras Belong in the Courtroom," *USA Today*, July 1996.
George J. Bryjak	"We Believe in Death Penalty but Shrink from Watching," *National Catholic Reporter*, May 18, 2001.
William F. Buckley Jr.	"Watch the Killer Get Killed?" *National Review*, May 28, 2001.
Economist	"Law and the Media: You're Under Arrest, and on TV," March 27, 1999.
Economist	"Television on Trial," December 19, 1998.
Walter Goodman	"Court TV and the Case of the Curious Witnesses," *New York Times*, July 21, 1997.
Timothy Noah	"Why Is TV in a Jury Room?" *U.S. News & World Report*, April 21, 1997.
Frank Rich	"Death with Commercials," *New York Times*, June 23, 2001.
Howard Rosenberg	"Are We Truly a Nation of Voyeurs, as It Seems?" *Los Angeles Times*, July 3, 2000.
Howard Rosenberg	"Let's Bring Cameras to Death's Door," *Los Angeles Times*, August 4, 1997.
Stan Statham	"Dead Man Watching," *Vital Speeches of the Day*, July 1, 2001.
Andrew Sullivan	"Watch It," *New Republic*, April 30, 2001.

For Further Discussion

Chapter 1

1. Robert S. Peck is a member and senior director of the Association of Trial Lawyers of America. Do you think his position biases his argument against tort reform, or do you believe it makes his criticism of such legislation more effective? Explain your answers.

2. After reading the viewpoints by John H. Church Jr. and Deborah R. Hensler et al., do you feel that class-action suits benefit lawyers or clients? Why?

3. Max Boot asserts that activist judges are harmful to democracy. Assuming his assertion is correct, what steps should be taken to ensure that judges do not let their political views take over their legal opinions? Explain your answers.

Chapter 2

1. In his viewpoint in favor of jury nullification, Nathan Lapp maintains that nullification has been part of the American jury system for more than three centuries. Nancy King contends that jurors throughout history have used nullification to support their racist views. How do their arguments affect your views on whether jury nullification should be permitted? Explain your answer.

2. After reading the viewpoints by Gregory E. Mize and Bobby Lee Cook and Michael A. Sullivan, do you think that it is possible for diverse and impartial juries to be selected? If not, should peremptory challenges be disallowed or can other steps be taken? Why or why not?

3. After reading the viewpoints in this chapter, do you believe the American jury system should be reformed? If so, what steps do you think would be most effective and why?

Chapter 3

1. In his argument against racial profiling, David A. Harris argues that pretextual traffic stops damage the credibility of the criminal justice system. However, John Derbyshire asserts that police stop and question minorities because of negative but accurate stereotypes. After reading their viewpoints, what is your opinion on these traffic stops? Are law enforcement officers justified in their actions? Explain your answers.

2. One argument against mandatory minimum drug sentences, as noted by Maxine Waters, is that such sentences eliminate judi-

cial discretion. In his viewpoint in favor of mandatory minimums, George Allen contends that these sentences reflect the desires of most Americans. Do you believe that sentencing, whether for drug possession or other crimes, should be based on a judge's interpretation of the laws or on public opinion? What are the advantages and disadvantages to both approaches? Explain your answers.

3. Laurence H. Tribe and Wendy Kaminer disagree on the need for a victims' rights amendment. Do you believe that such an amendment would prevent a defendant from receiving a fair trial, or would it properly acknowledge the role of victims in the criminal justice system? Explain your answers, drawing from the viewpoints and any other relevant material.

Chapter 4

1. After reading the viewpoints by Fred Graham and Woody West, do you think that cameras should be allowed in courtrooms? Why or why not?

2. In his argument for televising the death penalty, Thomas Lynch asserts that public airings of executions will compel Americans to determine the value of capital punishment. Raymond A. Schroth decries the shock value of televised executions. Do you believe that televised executions would be enlightening or sensationalist? Explain your answer.

3. The authors in this chapter consider the effects of the media, in particular television, on the legal system. Based on the viewpoints and any additional readings, do you feel that the media have had a positive or negative impact on the legal system? How can media coverage be improved? Explain your answers.

Organizations to Contact

The editors have compiled the following list of organizations concerned with issues debated in this book. The descriptions are derived from materials provided by the organizations. All have publications or information available for interested readers. The list was compiled on the date of publication of the present volume; the information provided here may change. Be aware that many organizations take several weeks or longer to respond to inquiries, so allow as much time as possible.

American Bar Association (ABA)
740 15th St. NW, Washington, DC 20005
(202) 662-1000
e-mail: service@abanet.org • website: www.abanet.org
The ABA is the world's largest voluntary professional association. Its mission is to represent the legal profession on a national level and serve the public by promoting justice and respect for the law. The ABA achieves its goals by providing law school accreditation, programs to assist judges and lawyers, and initiatives to improve the legal system. Its publications include the monthly *ABA Journal* and the quarterly magazine *Criminal Justice*.

American Tort Reform Association (ATRA)
1850 M St. NW, Suite 1095, Washington, DC 20036
(202) 682-1163 • fax: (202) 682-1022
website: www.atra.org
The ATRA is a bipartisan coalition of more than three hundred businesses, municipalities, and associations, who advocate tort reform in order to make the civil justice system fairer and more efficient. Among the ATRA-supported tort reforms that have become law in forty-five states and the District of Columbia are comprehensive product liability reforms and penalties on parties who bring frivolous lawsuits. The ATRA publishes the quarterly newsletter *Reformer*.

Association of Trial Lawyers of America (ATLA)
Leonard M. Ring Law Center
1050 31st St. NW, Washington, DC 20007
(800) 424-2725 • fax: (202) 298-6849
e-mail: info@atlahq.org • website: www.atlanet.org
The goal of the ATLA is to strengthen the civil justice system through education. ATLA also promotes trial by jury and justice

and fairness for injured persons. ATLA publishes the monthly magazine *Trial*.

Center for Law and Social Policy (CLASP)
1616 P St. NW, Suite 150, Washington, DC 20036
(202) 328-5140 • fax: (202) 328-5195
e-mail: info@clasp.org • website: www.clasp.org
CLASP is a national nonprofit organization that uses education, research, and advocacy to strengthen access for low-income persons to the civil justice system. The organization also aims to improve the economic security of low-income families. Publications include *Civil Legal Assistance for the Twenty-First Century: Achieving Equal Justice for All* and *Can Legal Services Achieve Equal Justice?*

Citizens Against Lawsuit Abuse (CALA)
3128 Pacific Coast Hwy., Suite 15, Torrance, CA 90505
(213) 630-1176 (outside California)
(800) 293-CALA (California only)
e-mail: mail-list@cala.com • website: www.cala.com
CALA is a nonprofit organization whose mission is to educate the public on the impact of lawsuit abuse, encourage debate on civil justice reform, and act as a watchdog over people and interest groups who seek to abuse the legal system. CALA publishes newsletters and press releases.

Families Against Mandatory Minimums (FAMM)
1612 K St. NW, Suite 1400, Washington, DC 20006
(202) 822-6700
e-mail: famm@famm.org • website: www.famm.org
FAMM is a national organization of citizens working to improve sentencing guidelines and reform mandatory sentencing laws that remove judicial discretion. The organization uses media outreach, direct action, and grassroots campaigns to educate the public and policy makers about mandatory minimums. FAMM publishes the quarterly newsletter *FAMMGram*.

Fully Informed Jury Association (FIJA)
PO Box 59, Helmville, MT 59843
(406) 793-5550 • fax: (406) 793-5550
e-mail: webforeman@fija.org • website: www.fija.org
The FIJA is dedicated to educating Americans about their rights, powers, and responsibilities as trial jurors. FIJA believes that the power of the jury is to judge not only the evidence but also the merits of the law. The organization publishes the quarterly newsletter *FIJActivist*.

HALT
1612 K St. NW, Suite 510, Washington, DC 20006
(888) FOR-HALT • fax (202) 887-9699
e-mail: halt@halt.org • website: www.halt.org
HALT is the nation's largest and oldest legal reform organization. The organization believes that Americans should be able to handle their legal affairs simply, affordably, and equitably. In addition to its newsletter *Legal Reformer*, HALT provides self-help books, including *Using a Lawyer . . . and What to Do If Things Go Wrong* and *Do-It-Yourself Law*, and public educational materials to help citizens understand the legal process and manage their legal affairs.

Justice Fellowship
PO Box 16069, Washington, DC 20041-6069
(703) 456-4050 • fax (703) 478-9679
e-mail: mail@justicefellowship.org
website: www.justicefellowship.org
Justice Fellowship is a nonprofit public policy organization dedicated to advancing biblically based restorative justice principles throughout the United States. It advocates restitution and reconciliation and the right of victims to play a meaningful role in the criminal justice process. Its publications include the book *Restoring Justice* and the bimonthly *Justice Report*.

National Association of Blacks in Criminal Justice
North Carolina Central University
PO Box 19788, Durham, NC 27707
(919) 683-1801 • fax: (919) 683-1903
e-mail: office@nabcj.org • website: www.nabcj.org
The National Association of Blacks in Criminal Justice is a multiethnic, nonpartisan, and nonprofit association of criminal justice professionals and community leaders. The association focuses its attention on law enforcement, the courts, and crime prevention, as well as the welfare and influence of minorities in the justice system. The association publishes the newsletter *Commitment*.

National Institute of Justice (NIJ)
810 Seventh St. NW, Washington, DC 20531
(202) 307-2942 • fax: (202) 307-6394
e-mail: askncjrs@ncjrs.org • website: www.ojp.usdoj.gov/nij
The NIJ is the research and development agency of the U.S. Department of Justice and is the only federal agency solely dedicated to researching crime control and justice issues. NIJ provides objective, independent, nonpartisan, evidence-based knowledge and

tools to meet the challenges of crime and justice, particularly at the state and local levels. Publications include the research briefs "Sentencing Guidelines: Reflections on the Future" and "The Rights of Crime Victims—Does Legal Protection Make a Difference?" and the monthly magazine *National Institute of Justice Journal*.

Rand Institute for Civil Justice

1700 Main St., PO Box 2138, Santa Monica, CA 90407-2138
fax: (310) 451-6979
e-mail: zakaras@rand.org • website: www.rand.org/icj

The Institute for Civil Justice is an independent research program whose mission is to help make the civil justice system fairer and more efficient. The organization analyzes trends and outcomes and evaluates solutions to policy problems. Its publications include *Punitive Damage Awards in Financial Injury Jury Verdicts* and *Do We Need an Empirical Research Agenda on Judicial Independence?*

Sentencing Project

514 10th St. NW, Suite 1000, Washington, DC 20004
(202) 628-0871 • fax: (202) 628-1091
e-mail: staff@sentencingproject.org
website: www.sentencingproject.org

The Sentencing Project is a national leader in the development of alternative sentencing programs and in the reform of criminal justice policy. It provides data, criminal justice policy analysis, and other resources for the public, media, and policy makers. The project publishes fact sheets, briefings, and reports, including *Young Black Men and the Criminal Justice System* and *Does the Punishment Fit the Crime?*

United States Sentencing Commission

One Columbus Circle NE, Washington, DC 20002-8002
(202) 502-4500
e-mail: pubaffairs@ussc.gov • website:www.ussc.gov

The United States Sentencing Commission is an independent federal agency that collects data about crime and sentencing and helps develop guidelines for sentencing in federal courts. The commission also trains criminal justice professionals in the use of the guidelines and serves as a clearinghouse of crime and sentencing information for the federal government, criminal justice professionals, and the public. The commission publishes annual reports, occasional newsletters, and reports to Congress, including *Special Report to the Congress: Cocaine and Federal Sentencing Policy*.

Bibliography of Books

Anthony G. Amsterdam and Jerome Bruner — *Minding the Law*. Cambridge, MA: Harvard University Press, 2000.

Max Boot — *Out of Order: Arrogance, Corruption, and Incompetence on the Bench*. New York: BasicBooks, 1998.

Matthew D. Bunker — *Justice and the Media: Reconciling Fair Trials and a Free Press*. Mahwah, NJ: Erlbaum, 1997.

Paul F. Campos — *Jurismania: The Madness of American Law*. New York: Oxford University Press, 1998.

Norman F. Cantor — *Imagining the Law: Common Law and the Foundations of the American Legal System*. New York: HarperCollins, 1997.

Jonathan P. Caulkins et al. — *Mandatory Minimum Drug Sentences: Throwing Away the Key or the Taxpayers' Money?* Santa Monica, CA: Rand, 1997.

Anthony Chase — *Law and History: The Evolution of the American Legal System*. New York: New Press, 1997.

Lloyd Chiasson Jr., ed. — *The Press on Trial: Crimes and Trials as Media Events*. Westport, CT: Greenwood Press, 1997.

Marjorie Cohn and David Dow — *Cameras in the Courtroom: Television and the Pursuit of Justice*. Jefferson, NC: McFarland, 1998.

David Cole — *No Equal Justice: Race and Class in the American Criminal Justice System*. New York: New Press, 1999.

William J. Cornelius — *Swift and Sure: Bringing Certainty and Finality to Criminal Punishments*. Irvington-on-Hudson, NY: Bridge Street Books, 1997.

Jay M. Feinman — *Law 101: Everything You Need to Know About the American Legal System*. New York: Oxford University Press, 2000.

Harvey Fireside — *The Fifth Amendment: The Right to Remain Silent*. Springfield, NJ: Enslow, 1998.

Richard L. Fox and Robert W. Van Sickel — *Tabloid Justice: Criminal Justice in an Age of Media Frenzy*. Boulder, CO: Lynne Rienner, 2001.

Patrick M. Garry — *A Nation of Adversaries: How the Litigation Explosion Is Reshaping America*. New York: Plenum Press, 1997.

Laurence H. Geller and Peter Hemenway — *Last Chance for Justice: The Juror's Lonely Quest*. Dallas: NCDS Press, 1997.

Robert Giles and
Robert W. Snyder, eds.
Covering the Courts: Free Press, Fair Trials, and Journalistic Performance. New Brunswick, NJ: Transaction Publishers, 1999.

Ronald L. Goldfarb
TV or Not TV: Television, Justice, and the Courts. New York: New York University Press, 1998.

Deborah R. Hensler et al.
Class Action Dilemmas: Pursuing Public Goals for Private Gain: Executive Summary. Santa Monica, CA: Rand Institute for Civil Justice, 1999.

Randall Kennedy
Race, Crime, and the Law. New York: Pantheon Books, 1997.

Richard S. Markovits
Matters of Principle: Legitimate Legal Argument and Constitutional Interpretation. New York: New York University Press, 1998.

Marilyn McShane and Frank P. Williams III, eds.
The American Court System. New York: Garland, 1997.

Gail Williams O'Brien
The Color of the Law: Race, Violence, and Justice in the Post–World War II South. Chapel Hill: University of North Carolina Press, 1999.

William T. Pizzi
Trials Without Truth: Why Our System of Criminal Trials Has Become an Expensive Failure and What We Need to Do to Rebuild It. New York: New York University Press, 1999.

Frank Schmalleger
Criminal Justice: A Brief Introduction. Upper Saddle River, NJ: Prentice-Hall, 1997.

Benjamin Sells
Order in the Court: Crafting a More Just World in Lawless Times. Boston: Element Books, 1999.

Barry Siegel
Actual Innocence. New York: Ballantine Books, 1999.

James Q. Wilson
Moral Judgment: Does the Abuse Excuse Threaten Our Legal System? New York: BasicBooks, 1997.

Index